HOW TO START YOUR OWN PARTY PLANNING BUSINESS

BusinessBookstore.com

About BusinessBookstore.com

Since 2002, BusinessBookstore.com has been dedicated to helping entrepreneurs turn their dreams into reality. With over 120,000 customers served, our mission is to empower small businesses by offering practical guidance and resources. Whether you're starting a new business, seeking a second income, or aiming to boost your existing business's profitability, we provide the tools and expertise you need.

Founded by lifelong entrepreneur **Terry Allan "Blake"**, BusinessBookstore.com leverages decades of hands-on business experience. Blake's entrepreneurial journey began at 19, and he has successfully built, grown, and sold multiple businesses since then. His passion for entrepreneurship and helping others led to the creation of BusinessBookstore.com, where he shares valuable insights through comprehensive books and resources.

Hunter Allan Blake joined his father in 2020, bringing his creative talents as the Editor and Illustrator. His skills ensure our content is visually engaging and easy to understand, enhancing the overall experience for our readers.

BusinessBookstore.com specialize in high-quality books and business plans available in digital formats and hard copy. Each resource is designed to simplify the business process, offering step-by-step instructions and expert insights tailored to entrepreneurs at every stage.

Our goal is to help you avoid a life spent away from your loved ones, stuck in a job that doesn't inspire you. Each morning, we want you to feel motivated to work on your dreams, not someone else's. We're committed to guiding you with easy-to-follow steps through your journey. Let's make your dreams a reality together, from one entrepreneur to another.

Go to: www.businessbookstore.com/start
to download blank templates for your business.

Available Resources

- Blank Templates
- Checklists
- Blog Articles
- Special Offers

- Video Tutorials
- Courses
- Links to Suppliers
- List of Franchises

Book ID: B064-6626

Introduction

Welcome to **How to Start Your Own Party Planning Business**, a comprehensive workbook designed specifically for aspiring entrepreneurs like you who are ready to turn their passion for planning into a thriving business. Whether you're dreaming of organizing extravagant weddings, intimate gatherings, corporate events, or unforgettable birthday parties, this book will guide you every step of the way. The event planning industry is booming, with the global market expected to reach over $1,135 billion by 2026, growing at a compound annual growth rate (CAGR) of 11.2%. Now is the perfect time to dive into this exciting field!

This workbook is not just a collection of information; it's a hands-on resource filled with actionable activities, checklists, and templates that will help you put theory into practice. Each chapter is designed to build upon the last, leading you through the essential stages of starting your own Party Planning Business. From defining your vision and setting goals to understanding your target audience and developing your marketing strategy, you will gain the knowledge and tools necessary to create a successful business.

As you embark on this journey, you will learn how to:

- **Set clear goals** that align with your vision and motivate you to overcome challenges.

- **Conduct market research** to understand trends and customer preferences, ensuring your services meet the needs of your target audience.

- **Identify your ideal clients** by creating customer personas that reflect their demographics, interests, and pain points.

- **Evaluate franchise options** if you're considering a structured path to entrepreneurship.

- **Analyze your competition** to identify strengths and weaknesses, allowing you to carve out your unique position in the market.

- **Estimate startup costs** and project revenues, giving you a clear financial roadmap for your business.

- **Choose the right legal structure** for your business, ensuring compliance and protection.

- **Craft a compelling business plan** that outlines your vision, market analysis, and marketing strategy.

- **Establish your online presence** through a professional website and engaging social media profiles.

- **Implement effective marketing strategies** that resonate with your audience and drive sales.

Each chapter concludes with an activity designed to reinforce what you've learned and to encourage you to apply it directly to your business. By the end of this workbook, you will have a well-defined plan and the confidence to launch your Party Planning Business.

Remember, every successful business starts with a single step. With dedication, creativity, and the right guidance, you can turn your passion for party planning into a rewarding career. Let's get started on your exciting journey toward entrepreneurship!

Table of Contents

——— PLAN YOUR BUSINESS ———

START YOUR BUSINESS

PROMOTE YOUR BUSINESS

Plan Your Business

Chapter 1

Vision and Motivation

Key Takeaways

- Purpose: Key to Motivation & Resilience

- Goal Setting for Store Success

- Activity: Purpose Reflection

- Activity: Goal Setting Exercise

Welcome to the first chapter of your journey toward starting your own Party Planning Business! In this section, we will explore the essential elements of **vision** and **motivation** that will serve as the foundation for your entrepreneurial adventure. As you embark on this path, it's crucial to cultivate a clear vision of what you want to achieve and to understand the driving forces behind your aspirations.

Every successful business begins with a compelling vision. This vision not only defines your goals but also inspires you to overcome challenges and stay focused on your objectives. When you can visualize your success, you're more likely to take the necessary steps to make it a reality. This chapter is designed to help you articulate that vision and set meaningful goals that align with it.

Motivation plays a pivotal role in your journey. It will fuel your passion, push you through obstacles, and keep you dedicated to your business. Understanding your purpose—why you want to start this business—will provide you with the resilience needed to navigate the ups and downs of entrepreneurship. As you reflect on your motivations, you'll find a deeper connection to your work, making it easier to stay committed.

Throughout this chapter, you will engage in activities that will help you clarify your goals and reflect on your purpose. By the end, you will have a strong foundation to build upon as you move forward in the exciting world of party planning. Remember, every great achievement starts with a vision, and the journey to realizing that vision begins with you!

Purpose: Key to Motivation & Resilience

Understanding your purpose is a fundamental aspect of starting and sustaining a successful Party Planning Business. Purpose acts as the driving force behind your actions, influencing your decisions, and ultimately shaping your resilience in the face of challenges. When you have a clear sense of purpose, it becomes easier to stay motivated, even when the going gets tough.

Your purpose is not just about what you do; it's about why you do it. For instance, if your goal is to create memorable experiences for clients, your purpose might revolve around the joy of bringing people together and creating lasting memories. This deeper understanding can guide your business decisions, from the types of events you choose to plan to the way you interact with clients and suppliers.

Here are some ways to explore and articulate your purpose:

- **Reflect on Your Passion:** Consider what aspects of party planning excite you the most. Is it the creativity involved in designing themes, the logistics of coordinating events, or the satisfaction of seeing clients happy? Identifying your passion can help clarify your purpose.

- **Identify Your Values:** What values are important to you? Integrity, creativity, and customer satisfaction are examples of values that can inform your purpose. Aligning your business with your values can lead to more authentic interactions and a stronger connection with your clients.

- **Consider Your Impact:** Think about the impact you want to have on your clients and community. Do you want to support local businesses by sourcing materials and services locally? Do you aim to promote sustainability in your events? Understanding your desired impact can help shape your purpose.

Once you have a clearer understanding of your purpose, it's essential to document it. A well-articulated purpose statement can serve as a motivational tool, reminding you of your "why" during challenging times. For example, you might write:

"My purpose is to create unforgettable experiences that bring people together, foster joy, and celebrate life's milestones, all while supporting local vendors and promoting sustainable practices."

This statement not only defines your purpose but can also act as a guiding principle for your business operations and marketing strategies.

Moreover, a strong sense of purpose contributes to resilience. Entrepreneurship is filled with ups and downs, and having a clear purpose can help you navigate through difficult times. When faced with setbacks—be it a canceled event, a dissatisfied client, or financial hurdles—your purpose can serve as a reminder of why you started this journey in the first place. It can motivate you to find solutions rather than succumb to despair.

In conclusion, understanding your purpose is key to maintaining motivation and resilience in your Party Planning Business. Take the time to explore your passions, identify your values, and consider the impact you want to make. Document your purpose statement and use it as a touchstone for your business journey. With a clear purpose, you'll find it easier to stay motivated, overcome challenges, and ultimately thrive in your entrepreneurial endeavors.

Goal Setting for Success

Setting clear and achievable goals is a fundamental step in establishing a successful Party Planning Business. Goals provide direction, focus, and a benchmark for measuring progress. They help you clarify your vision and motivate you to take actionable steps toward your objectives.

When setting goals, it's essential to use the SMART criteria, which stands for:

- **Specific:** Your goals should be clear and specific, answering the questions of what, why, and how. For example, instead of saying "I want to be successful," a specific goal would be "I want to plan 10 events in my first year."

- **Measurable:** Ensure that your goals can be quantified or measured. This allows you to track your progress. For instance, "I will increase my client base by 20% within six months" is measurable.

- **Achievable:** Your goals should be realistic and attainable. Consider your resources and constraints when setting these goals. For example, "I will attend two local networking events each month" is achievable if you have the time and resources to do so.

- **Relevant:** Goals should align with your overall business objectives and values. For example, if your business focuses on eco-friendly events, a relevant goal might be "I will partner with three sustainable vendors within the next year."

- **Time-bound:** Set a deadline for your goals to encourage urgency and commitment. For example, "I will complete my business plan by the end of this month" gives you a clear timeframe.

Another effective approach to goal setting is to differentiate between short-term and long-term goals. Short-term goals are those you can achieve within a few weeks or months, while long-term goals may take a year or more to accomplish. Here's how you can structure them:

- **Short-term Goals:**

  - Complete a market research survey within the next two weeks.

  - Attend one networking event this month.

  - Create a social media profile for your business within the next week.

- **Long-term Goals:**

  - Establish a solid client base of 50 clients within three years.

  - Expand services to include corporate event planning within five years.

  - Achieve a revenue target of $100,000 in the first three years.

Once you have established your goals, it's crucial to document them. Writing down your goals not only reinforces your commitment but also serves as a reminder of what you are working towards. Consider creating a vision board or a goal journal where you can visualize and track your progress.

Lastly, remember that goal setting is an ongoing process. As you achieve your goals, take time to reassess and set new ones. This adaptability will keep your business dynamic and responsive to changes in the market or your personal aspirations.

In summary, effective goal setting is a powerful tool that can guide you on your journey to starting a successful Party Planning Business. By applying the SMART criteria, distinguishing between short-term and long-term goals, and regularly reviewing your objectives, you'll be well-equipped to navigate the challenges and opportunities ahead.

Visit **www.BusinessBookstore.com/start** to download blank forms, etc.

Activity: Purpose Reflection

In this activity, you'll have the opportunity to reflect on the deeper purpose driving your entrepreneurial venture. Take some time to consider why you started your own business and the impact you hope to make in the world through your business. After reflecting on these questions, jot down your thoughts and insights in the space provided below.

Instructions:

1. Find a quiet and comfortable space where you can reflect without distractions.

2. Take a few deep breaths to center yourself and clear your mind.

3. Reflect on the following questions:

- What inspired you to start your own business?

- What values and principles do you want your business to embody?

- How do you envision your business making a positive impact in the world?

- What legacy do you hope to leave through your entrepreneurial journey?

4. Write down your responses in the space provided below.

_____

_____

_____

5. Once you've completed your reflection, take a moment to review your answers and consider how they align with your vision for your business.

Purpose Reflection:

1. What inspired you to start your own business?

2. What values and principles do you want your business to embody?

3. How do you envision your business making a positive impact in the world?

4. What legacy do you hope to leave through your entrepreneurial journey?

5. Additional Notes or Insights:

_____

_____

_____

Take your time to reflect deeply on these questions, and don't hesitate to revisit them periodically as your business evolves. Your sense of purpose is a powerful driver of motivation and resilience on your entrepreneurial journey, so embrace it, nurture it, and let it guide you towards success in the dynamic world of business.

Goal Setting Exercise

Now that we've explored the importance of goal setting in Chapter 1, it's time to put theory into practice and define clear objectives for your business. Below, you'll find a goal-setting exercise designed to help you articulate your goals and create a roadmap for success. Remember to be specific, measurable, achievable, relevant, and time-bound (SMART) when setting your goals.

Business Information

- Business Name: _____
- Owners Name: _____
- Date: _____

Vision Statement

Describe the long term vision for your business

_____
_____
_____
_____

Mission Statement

State the purpose of your business and its core values.

_____
_____
_____
_____

List of Goals

Write down each goal you want to accomplish. Consider goals related to growth, revenue, community impact, etc.

☑	GOALS	PRIORITY
☐		(H) (M) (L)
☐		(H) (M) (L)
☐		(H) (M) (L)
☐		(H) (M) (L)
☐		(H) (M) (L)
☐		(H) (M) (L)
☐		(H) (M) (L)
☐		(H) (M) (L)
☐		(H) (M) (L)
☐		(H) (M) (L)
☐		(H) (M) (L)

For each goal listed, assign a priority level of High, Medium, or Low based on its importance and urgency in achieving your overall vision.

- **High Priority:** Goals that are crucial to your immediate success and long-term sustainability.

- **Medium Priority:** Goals that are important but may not require immediate attention.

- **Low Priority:** Goals that are less urgent or can be deferred to a later time.

Goal Details

Take your high priority goal and rewrite it to include specific details and measurable outcomes. Ensure clarity in what you aim to accomplish and how success will be defined.

Key Motivations

Write down the reasons why this goal is important to you. Consider how achieving this goal aligns with your vision, values, and overall business objectives.

Actionable Tasks

Break down the goal into actionable tasks and steps that need to be completed to achieve it. Prioritize these tasks based on their importance and sequence them in a logical order to ensure smooth progress towards achieving the goal.

By following these steps, you'll effectively structure and prioritize your goals, and develop detailed plans for achieving your high priority objectives. This systematic approach will help you stay focused, motivated, and on track towards building a successful business.

Goal Details

Take your high priority goal and rewrite it to include specific details and measurable outcomes. Ensure clarity in what you aim to accomplish and how success will be defined.

_____

_____

_____

_____

Key Motivations

Write down the reasons why this goal is important to you. Consider how achieving this goal aligns with your vision, values, and overall business objectives.

_____

_____

_____

Actionable Tasks

Break down the goal into actionable tasks and steps that need to be completed to achieve it. Prioritize these tasks based on their importance and sequence them in a logical order to ensure smooth progress towards achieving the goal.

_____

_____

_____

_____

_____

_____

_____

By following these steps, you'll effectively structure and prioritize your goals, and develop detailed plans for achieving your high priority objectives. This systematic approach will help you stay focused, motivated, and on track towards building a successful business.

Goal Details

Take your high priority goal and rewrite it to include specific details and measurable outcomes. Ensure clarity in what you aim to accomplish and how success will be defined.

_____

_____

_____

_____

Key Motivations

Write down the reasons why this goal is important to you. Consider how achieving this goal aligns with your vision, values, and overall business objectives.

_____

_____

_____

Actionable Tasks

Break down the goal into actionable tasks and steps that need to be completed to achieve it. Prioritize these tasks based on their importance and sequence them in a logical order to ensure smooth progress towards achieving the goal.

_____

_____

_____

_____

_____

_____

_____

By following these steps, you'll effectively structure and prioritize your goals, and develop detailed plans for achieving your high priority objectives. This systematic approach will help you stay focused, motivated, and on track towards building a successful business.

Review and Reflect

Regularly review your goals, reflect on your progress, and make adjustments as needed.

- **Date of Review:** _____
- **Progress Summary:** _____
- **Challenges Faced:** _____
- **Adjustments Needed:** _____

Visit **www.BusinessBookstore.com/start** to download blank goal forms.

Chapter 2

Conduct Market Research

Key Takeaways

- Understanding Market Trends

- Analyzing Customer Needs and Preferences

- Activity: Market Research Survey Template

Welcome to Chapter 2: Conduct Market Research! As you embark on the exciting journey of starting your own Party Planning Business, understanding the market landscape is crucial to your success. Market research is not just a step in the process; it is the foundation upon which you will build your business. By gathering insights about trends, customer preferences, and competitors, you will be well equipped to make informed decisions that align with your goals.

In this chapter, you will learn how to:

- Identify current market trends that can impact your business.

- Analyze customer needs and preferences to tailor your services effectively.

- Gather and interpret data to create a competitive advantage.

Market research may seem daunting, but it is an empowering tool that can help you connect with your audience and refine your offerings. Remember, knowledge is power! The more you understand your market, the better you can position your business to meet the demands of your potential clients.

As you engage in the activities outlined in this chapter, keep an open mind and be willing to adapt your ideas based on what you discover. This process will not only enhance your business strategy but also boost your confidence as you move forward. Embrace the learning experience, and remember that every piece of information you gather will bring you one step closer to realizing your entrepreneurial dreams.

Let's dive in and begin conducting your market research!

Understanding Market Trends

Understanding market trends is crucial for anyone looking to start a Party Planning Business. Market trends refer to the general direction in which a particular market is moving over time. By analyzing these trends, you can identify opportunities, anticipate challenges, and make informed decisions that will help your business thrive.

To effectively understand market trends, consider the following key areas:

- **Industry Growth:** Research the overall growth of the party planning industry. Look for statistics on revenue growth, employment rates, and the number of businesses entering the market. For instance, according to industry reports, the event planning market has seen significant growth in recent years, driven by increased consumer spending on events and experiences.

- **Consumer Behavior:** Analyze how consumer preferences are changing. Are people leaning towards more personalized and unique experiences? For example, many clients are now favoring eco-friendly events or themed parties that reflect their personal interests. Understanding these shifts can help you tailor your services to meet customer demands.

- **Technological Advancements:** Stay updated on the latest technology trends that can impact party planning. Tools like event management software, virtual reality for event experiences, and social media platforms for marketing are becoming increasingly popular. For example, using platforms like Eventbrite or Meetup can help you reach a broader audience and streamline your event management processes.

- **Seasonal Trends:** Different times of the year can influence the types of events people plan. For instance, wedding season typically peaks in the summer months, while corporate events may be more prevalent in the fall. Understanding these seasonal trends can help you prepare your marketing strategies and service offerings accordingly.

- **Competitive Landscape:** Keep an eye on your competitors and their offerings. What services are they providing? Are there gaps in the market that you can fill? Analyzing your competition can give you insights into what is currently trending and help you differentiate your business.

To gather information on these trends, utilize a variety of resources:

- **Industry Reports:** Organizations like IBISWorld or Statista provide comprehensive reports on industry trends that can be invaluable for your research.

- **Surveys and Polls:** Conduct your surveys or utilize existing ones to gather data on consumer preferences and behaviors. This can provide direct insights into what potential clients are looking for.

- **Networking:** Attend industry conferences, trade shows, and networking events to connect with other professionals. Engaging with peers can offer firsthand knowledge about emerging trends and best practices.

- **Social Media and Online Forums:** Platforms like LinkedIn, Facebook groups, or industry-specific forums can be excellent sources for gauging consumer sentiment and discovering new trends.

In conclusion, understanding market trends is not just about keeping up with what's popular; it's about anticipating the future needs of your clients and adapting your business strategies accordingly. By staying informed and proactive, you can position your Party Planning Business for success in a competitive landscape.

Analyzing Customer Needs and Preferences

Understanding customer needs and preferences is crucial for any successful Party Planning Business. By analyzing what your potential clients desire, you can tailor your services to meet their expectations, ensuring satisfaction and repeat business. Here are some key steps to effectively analyze customer needs and preferences:

1. **Conduct Surveys and Questionnaires**: One of the most direct ways to gather information about customer preferences is through surveys. You can create a simple questionnaire that asks potential clients about their party planning experiences, preferences, and expectations. Consider including questions such as:

   - What type of events do you typically organize (e.g., weddings, birthdays, corporate events)?

   - What is your budget range for party planning services?

   - What factors are most important to you when choosing a party planner (e.g., experience, creativity, pricing)?

Distributing these surveys through social media platforms, email newsletters, or during community events can yield valuable insights into your target market.

2. **Analyze Social Media Engagement**: Social media platforms are a treasure trove of information regarding customer interests and preferences. By observing which types of posts gain the most engagement (likes, shares, comments), you can identify trends and popular topics. For example:

   - If you notice that posts about themed parties receive a lot of attention, it may indicate a growing interest in that area.

   - Pay attention to comments and feedback on your posts, as they can provide insights into what your audience values.

3. **Focus Groups**: Hosting a focus group can provide in-depth insights into customer preferences. Invite a small group of potential clients to discuss their party planning experiences and expectations. This setting allows for open dialogue and can uncover nuanced insights that surveys may miss. Key questions to ask during a focus group include:

   - What do you find most challenging about planning a party?

   - What services do you wish party planners would offer that are currently lacking?

4. **Review Competitor Offerings**: Examining what your competitors offer can also shed light on customer preferences. Look at their services, pricing, and customer reviews. By understanding what works for them, you can identify gaps in the market or areas where you can differentiate your services. For instance:

   - If competitors frequently receive praise for their unique themes, consider how you can incorporate innovative themes into your offerings.

   - Analyze customer feedback on competitors' social media pages or review sites to gauge what clients appreciate or dislike.

5. **Leverage Customer Feedback**: Once you start your business, actively seek and encourage feedback from your clients. After every event, send a follow-up email asking for their thoughts on your services. This will not only help you improve but also show clients that you value their opinions. You might ask:

   - What aspects of the service did you find most beneficial?

   - Were there any areas where you felt we could improve?

By employing these strategies, you can gain a comprehensive understanding of customer needs and preferences, allowing you to create tailored services that resonate with your target audience. Remember, the more you understand your clients, the better equipped you will be to meet their expectations and build lasting relationships.

Visit **www.BusinessBookstore.com/start** to download blank forms, etc.

Activity: Market Research Survey Template

Now that you've learned about the importance of conducting market research and analyzing customer needs and preferences, it's time to put your knowledge into action. Use the following Market Research Survey Template to gather valuable insights from your target audience. This survey template includes topics discussed in this and previous chapters, helping you systematically collect data to inform your business decisions.

Instructions:

1. Review each question in the survey template carefully.

2. Customize the survey to align with your business goals and target audience.

3. Distribute the survey to your target audience through email, social media, or other channels.

4. Collect and analyze the survey responses to identify trends, patterns, and actionable insights.

5. Use the insights gained from the survey to refine your business strategy, product offerings, and marketing initiatives.

Market Research Survey Template:

1. Demographic Information:

- Age: _____

- Gender: _____

- Location: _____

- Occupation: _____

2. Product/Service Usage:

- Have you used similar products/services in the past? (Yes/No)

- If yes, please specify the products/services you have used:

  _____

  _____

  _____

- What factors influenced your decision to use/not use these products/services?

  _____

  _____

  _____

3. Needs and Preferences:

- What are the primary needs or problems you seek to address when considering products/services in this category?

  _____

  _____

  _____

- What features or attributes are most important to you when choosing a product/service?

  _____

  _____

  _____

- How do you prefer to purchase or access products/services in this category? (In-store, online, mobile app, etc.)

  _____

  _____

  _____

4. Competitor Analysis:

- Are you aware of any competitors offering similar products/
  services? (Yes/No)

  _____

  _____

  _____

- If yes, please specify the competitors you are aware of:

  _____

  _____

  _____

- How would you compare the offerings of our business to those of
  our competitors?

  _____

  _____

  _____

5. Brand Perception:

- What comes to mind when you think of our brand/business?

  _____

  _____

  _____

- How would you describe the reputation or image of our brand/ business?

  _____

  _____

  _____

- What factors influence your perception of our brand/business positively or negatively?

  _____

  _____

  _____

6. Marketing and Communication Channels:

- How do you prefer to receive information about products/services in this category? (Email, social media, advertisements, etc.)

  _____

  _____

  _____

- Have you interacted with our brand/business through any marketing or communication channels? (Yes/No)

- If yes, please specify the channels you have interacted with:

  _____

  _____

  _____

7. Feedback and Suggestions:

- Do you have any additional feedback or suggestions for improving our products/services or customer experience?

  _____

  _____

  _____

Conclusion:

Completing the Market Research Survey Template provides valuable insights into the needs, preferences, and perceptions of your target audience. Use the findings to refine your business strategy, enhance your offerings, and better meet the needs of your customers. Remember, ongoing market research is essential for staying informed about evolving consumer trends and maintaining a competitive edge in the marketplace.

Chapter 3

Identify Your Target Audience

Key Takeaways

- Creating Customer Personas

- Conducting Audience Demographic Analysis

- Activity: Target Audience Persona Template

Welcome to Chapter 3: Identify Your Target Audience! As a small business owner, understanding your target audience is one of the most crucial steps in building a successful Party Planning Business. Knowing who your ideal clients are will help you tailor your services, marketing efforts, and customer interactions to meet their specific needs and preferences.

Your target audience is not just a demographic; they are the heart of your business. By identifying and understanding them, you can create memorable experiences that resonate with their desires. This chapter will guide you through the process of creating customer personas and conducting an audience demographic analysis, which will provide you with valuable insights into who your customers are and what they are looking for.

In today's competitive market, having a clear picture of your target audience can set you apart from the competition. It allows you to:

- **Tailor Your Marketing Efforts:** Direct your marketing campaigns to the right people at the right time.

- **Enhance Customer Engagement:** Create personalized experiences that foster loyalty and trust.

- **Improve Service Offerings:** Develop services that align with your audience's preferences and expectations.

As you dive into the activities in this chapter, remember that understanding your target audience is not a one-time task but an ongoing process. Stay curious, listen to feedback, and adapt your strategies as needed. By investing the time to truly know your audience, you are laying the foundation for a thriving Party Planning Business that meets the needs of your clients and stands out in the marketplace.

Creating Customer Personas

Creating customer personas is a critical step in understanding your target audience and tailoring your Party Planning Business to meet their specific needs. A customer persona is a semi-fictional representation of your ideal client based on market research and real data about your existing customers. By developing detailed personas, you can better align your services, marketing strategies, and overall business approach with what your clients truly want.

To create effective customer personas, follow these steps:

1. **Gather Data:** Start by collecting data from various sources. This can include:

    *   Surveys and questionnaires sent to past clients.

    *   Social media analytics to understand who is engaging with your content.

    *   Website analytics to see which demographics are visiting your site.

    *   Interviews with existing clients to gain insights into their preferences and motivations.

2. **Identify Key Characteristics:** Once you have gathered enough data, identify common characteristics among your clients. Consider the following attributes:

    *   *Demographics:* Age, gender, income level, education, and occupation.

    *   *Psychographics:* Interests, values, lifestyle choices, and personality traits.

    *   *Behavioral Traits:* Buying habits, preferred communication channels, and event preferences.

3. **Create Persona Profiles:** Based on the data and characteristics you've identified, create detailed persona profiles. Each profile should include:

- *Name:* Give your persona a name to make them relatable. For example, "Event Enthusiast Emily" or "Budget-Conscious Brian."

- *Background:* A brief description of their life situation, including their profession and family status.

- *Goals:* What do they hope to achieve with your services? This could include hosting a memorable birthday party, planning a corporate event, or organizing a wedding.

- *Challenges:* Identify the obstacles they face when planning events. For instance, they might struggle with time management, budgeting, or finding reliable vendors.

- *Preferred Communication:* How do they prefer to interact? Are they more likely to respond to emails, phone calls, or social media messages?

4. **Utilize Your Personas:** Once your customer personas are complete, use them to guide your business decisions. This can include:

- Tailoring your marketing messages to resonate with each persona.

- Offering services that specifically address the needs and challenges of your personas.

- Creating content that speaks directly to their interests and preferences.

For example, if you have a persona named "Luxury Lover Lisa," you might focus on high-end event planning services, premium vendor partnerships, and exclusive experiences that cater to her desire for elegance and sophistication. On the other hand, "DIY Dad Dan" might appreciate budget-friendly options and resources for planning events himself.

In conclusion, creating customer personas is an invaluable exercise that can significantly enhance your understanding of your target audience. By investing time in this process, you will be better equipped to tailor your services and marketing strategies, ultimately leading to a more successful Party Planning Business.

Conducting Audience Demographic Analysis

Understanding your target audience is crucial for the success of your Party Planning Business. Conducting a demographic analysis allows you to gather essential information about your potential clients, which can help you tailor your services to meet their needs effectively. In this section, we will explore the key components of demographic analysis and how to apply them in your business strategy.

Demographic analysis involves examining various characteristics of your audience, including:

- **Age:** Different age groups have distinct preferences and needs. For example, millennials may prefer trendy, themed parties, while baby boomers might favor more traditional celebrations.

- **Gender:** Understanding the gender distribution of your audience can influence the types of events you plan. For instance, bridal showers may attract a predominantly female audience, while corporate events might have a more balanced gender ratio.

- **Income Level:** The income level of your target audience will affect their spending habits. Higher-income clients may seek luxury services, while budget-conscious clients might look for cost-effective options.

- **Geographic Location:** Knowing where your audience is located can help you identify regional trends and preferences. For example, urban clients may prefer modern venues, while rural clients might lean towards outdoor events.

- **Education Level:** The education level of your audience can also influence their expectations and preferences. Highly educated clients may prioritize sophisticated themes and detailed planning.

To conduct a thorough demographic analysis, consider the following steps:

- **Gather Data:** Utilize surveys, online tools, and social media analytics to collect data about your audience. You can create an online survey using platforms like SurveyMonkey or Google Forms to gain insights into your potential clients' demographics.

- **Analyze Data:** Once you have collected the data, analyze it to identify trends and patterns. Look for common characteristics among your respondents that can inform your service offerings.

- **Create Customer Personas:** Based on your analysis, develop customer personas that represent your ideal clients. For example, a persona might be "Budget-Conscious Bride," who is 28 years old, lives in a suburban area, and has a moderate income. This persona can guide your marketing and service development.

- **Adjust Your Services:** Use the insights from your demographic analysis to tailor your services. If you find that many of your potential clients are young professionals, you might focus on creating trendy, upscale events that cater to their tastes.

In addition to these steps, consider leveraging existing market research reports and studies relevant to the party planning industry. Websites like IBISWorld or Statista can provide valuable insights into industry trends and consumer behavior.

Remember, demographic analysis is not a one-time task. Continuously gather feedback and update your analysis as your business grows and your audience evolves. By staying attuned to your target audience's demographics, you can position your Party Planning Business for success and create memorable experiences that resonate with your clients.

Activity: Target Audience Persona Template

Now that you've gathered insights about your target audience through demographic analysis and other research methods, it's time to create detailed customer personas. Use the following Target Audience Persona Template to develop personas that represent different segments of your audience. This template will help you humanize your audience and gain a deeper understanding of their needs, motivations, and preferences.

Instructions:

1. Review each section of the persona template carefully.

2. Fill in the details based on the insights and data you've gathered about your target audience.

3. Create multiple personas to represent distinct segments within your audience, if applicable.

4. Use the personas to inform your marketing strategies, product development, and customer engagement initiatives.

Target Audience Persona Template:

Persona Name: _____

Demographics:

- Age: _____

- Gender: _____

- Location: _____

- Occupation: _____

- Income Level: _____

- Education Level: _____

Background:

- Brief description of the persona's background and lifestyle.

  _____

  _____

  _____

- Family status (if applicable).

  _____

  _____

  _____

Goals and Objectives:

- Primary goals and objectives of the persona related to your product or service.

_____

_____

_____

- Secondary goals and aspirations.

_____

_____

_____

Challenges and Pain Points:

- Key challenges or pain points the persona faces in relation to your product or service.

_____

_____

_____

- Common obstacles or frustrations.

_____

_____

_____

Motivations and Values:

- Motivations and values that drive the persona's decision-making process.

_____

_____

_____

- What matters most to them in life and business.

_____

_____

_____

Behaviors and Preferences:

- Buying behaviors and preferences related to your product/service.

_____

_____

_____

- Preferred communication channels and media consumption habits.

_____

_____

_____

- Hobbies, interests, and lifestyle preferences.

_____

_____

_____

Quotes and Insights:

- Direct quotes or insights gathered from interviews, surveys, or observations.

_____

_____

_____

- What the persona says about your product or service.

_____

_____

_____

Conclusion:

Completing the Target Audience Persona Template provides you with a deeper understanding of the diverse needs and preferences of your target audience. Use the personas to tailor your strategies and initiatives to resonate with different audience segments effectively. Remember, personas are dynamic and should be updated regularly as you gather new insights and evolve your business strategies.

Chapter 4

Consider Buying a Franchise

Key Takeaways

- Exploring Franchise Opportunities

- Benefits and Challenges of Franchising

- Activity: Franchise Evaluation Checklist

As you embark on the journey of starting your own Party Planning Business, it's essential to explore all available avenues that can lead to success. One option that many aspiring entrepreneurs consider is buying a franchise. A franchise offers a unique blend of independence and support, allowing you to operate under a well-established brand while benefiting from a proven business model.

Franchising can be an excellent choice for those who may feel overwhelmed by the complexities of starting a business from scratch. With a franchise, you gain access to a network of resources, training, and ongoing support that can significantly ease the transition into entrepreneurship. This structured approach can be particularly advantageous in the competitive party planning industry, where brand recognition and established operational procedures can set you apart from the competition.

However, it's crucial to approach franchising with a clear understanding of its benefits and challenges. While the initial investment might be higher compared to starting an independent business, the potential for success often outweighs the costs. Franchises often come with a built-in customer base, marketing support, and a track record of success, which can accelerate your business growth.

In this chapter, we will delve into the world of franchising, exploring various opportunities, the advantages and challenges you may encounter, and how to evaluate whether a franchise is the right fit for your goals and aspirations. By the end of this chapter, you will be equipped with the knowledge needed to make an informed decision about whether franchising is the path for you on your journey to becoming a successful party planner.

Exploring Franchise Opportunities

Exploring franchise opportunities can be an appealing option for aspiring entrepreneurs in the Party Planning Business. A franchise allows you to operate under an established brand while benefiting from the support and resources provided by the franchisor. This section will guide you through the key aspects to consider when exploring franchise opportunities.

1. **Understanding Franchising**: Franchising is a business model where an individual (the franchisee) purchases the rights to operate a business under the name and system of an established company (the franchisor). The franchisee pays an initial franchise fee and ongoing royalties in exchange for the use of the brand, training, and support. In the party planning industry, franchises can range from event planning agencies to specialized services like party rental companies or themed party organizers.

2. **Benefits of Franchising**

   - **Established Brand Recognition:** One of the most significant advantages of franchising is the ability to leverage an established brand. This can lead to immediate customer trust and credibility.

   - **Comprehensive Training and Support:** Franchisees often receive extensive training and ongoing support from the franchisor, which can be invaluable for those new to the industry.

   - **Proven Business Model:** Franchises come with a tested business model, reducing the risks associated with starting a business from scratch.

   - **Marketing Assistance:** Many franchisors provide marketing materials and strategies to help franchisees attract customers and promote their services.

3. **Challenges of Franchising**

- **Initial Investment:** Franchise fees can be substantial, and there may be additional costs for equipment, inventory, and marketing.

- **Limited Flexibility:** Franchisees must adhere to the franchisor's guidelines and policies, which can limit creativity and operational flexibility.

- **Ongoing Royalties:** Franchisees are typically required to pay ongoing royalties, which can impact profitability.

4. **Researching Franchise Opportunities**: When considering a franchise in the party planning industry, it's essential to conduct thorough research to find the right fit for your goals and values. Here are some steps to guide you:

- **Identify Your Interests:** Determine what aspects of party planning you are most passionate about, such as event coordination, themed parties, or rentals.

- **Evaluate Franchise Options:** Look for franchises that align with your interests and have a solid reputation. Some popular party planning franchises include *Party City*, *Eventive*, and *Simply Elegant*.

- **Review Franchise Disclosure Documents (FDD):** The FDD provides crucial information about the franchise, including fees, obligations, and financial performance. Take the time to review this document carefully.

- **Speak with Current Franchisees:** Reach out to current franchisees to gain insights into their experiences, challenges, and successes. This can provide valuable information about the day-to-day operations and support from the franchisor.

- **Assess Financial Requirements:** Ensure you understand all financial commitments, including initial investment, ongoing fees, and potential revenue. Create a budget to evaluate if the franchise is financially viable for you.

5. **Making Your Decision**: After conducting thorough research and evaluating your options, take the time to reflect on your findings. Consider whether the franchise aligns with your personal goals, values, and financial situation. If you decide to move forward, consult with a legal or business advisor to ensure you understand all aspects of the franchise agreement.

Exploring franchise opportunities in the Party Planning Business can be a rewarding path for those seeking a structured approach to entrepreneurship. With the right research and preparation, you can find a franchise that not only meets your business aspirations but also allows you to thrive in this exciting industry.

Benefits and Challenges of Franchising

Franchising can be an appealing option for aspiring entrepreneurs looking to start a Party Planning Business. It offers a structured path to business ownership, but it also comes with its own set of benefits and challenges. Understanding these aspects is crucial for making an informed decision.

Benefits of Franchising

- **Established Brand Recognition:** One of the primary advantages of buying into a franchise is the ability to leverage an established brand. Customers are often more inclined to trust a recognized name, which can lead to quicker customer acquisition. For example, a franchise like *Party City* has built a reputation that can attract clients more rapidly than a new, independent business.

- **Proven Business Model:** Franchises typically come with a tried-and-tested business model. This means that the franchisee can benefit from operational procedures, marketing strategies, and customer service protocols that have been developed over time. This reduces the trial-and-error phase that many new businesses face.

- **Training and Support:** Most franchise systems offer comprehensive training programs and ongoing support. This can include everything from initial training on business operations to marketing guidance and customer service training. For instance, franchises like *Event Planning by Design* often provide workshops and resources to help franchisees succeed.

- **Collective Buying Power:** Franchisees often benefit from collective purchasing power, which can lead to lower costs for supplies and materials. This can be particularly advantageous in the Party Planning Business, where items such as decorations, catering supplies, and rental equipment can be expensive.

Challenges of Franchising

- **Initial Investment and Ongoing Fees:** While franchising can reduce some risks, it often requires a significant initial investment and ongoing royalty fees. Franchisees typically pay a percentage of their sales to the franchisor, which can cut into profits. It's essential to weigh these costs against the potential benefits.

- **Limited Creativity and Flexibility:** Franchise agreements often come with strict guidelines about how to operate the business. This can limit a franchisee's ability to innovate or adapt their services to local market demands. For example, if a franchise has a specific theme or style, a franchisee may not have the freedom to customize offerings for local events.

- **Dependency on Franchisor:** Franchisees are reliant on the franchisor for support, marketing, and brand reputation. If the franchisor faces challenges or makes poor business decisions, it can directly impact all franchisees. For instance, if a franchisor has a public relations issue, it may tarnish the reputation of all associated franchises.

- **Competition Among Franchisees:** In some cases, multiple franchise locations may operate in close proximity, leading to competition among franchisees. This can dilute market share and create tension within the franchise system.

In conclusion, while franchising can provide a valuable opportunity for individuals looking to enter the party planning industry, it is essential to thoroughly evaluate both the benefits and challenges. Conducting careful research and seeking advice from current franchisees can help potential business owners make a more informed decision about whether franchising is the right path for them.

Visit **www.BusinessBookstore.com/start** for a current list of franchises.

Activity: Franchise Evaluation Checklist

In this activity, you'll have the opportunity to evaluate franchise opportunities for your business using our Franchise Evaluation Checklist. This checklist will guide you through the key factors to consider when assessing franchise options, helping you make informed decisions about whether franchising is the right path for your business. Follow the instructions below to complete the Franchise Evaluation Checklist:

Check the appendix for a list of franchises.

Instructions:

1. **Review Franchise Criteria**: Consider the following criteria when evaluating franchise opportunities:

    ☐   Brand Recognition and Credibility

    ☐   Proven Business Model

    ☐   Initial Investment Costs

    ☐   Ongoing Fees and Royalties

    ☐   Support Services Provided by Franchisor

    ☐   Territory Rights and Restrictions

    ☐   Franchise Agreement Terms and Conditions

2. **Assess Franchise Opportunities**: Research and assess multiple franchise opportunities based on the criteria outlined above. Gather information from franchisors, franchise disclosure documents (FDDs), current franchisees, and other reliable sources.

3. **Complete Franchise Evaluation Checklist**: Use the checklist below to evaluate each franchise opportunity and determine its suitability for your movie theater business.

Franchise Evaluation Checklist:

1. **Brand Recognition and Credibility**:

   ☐ Established brand with strong market presence.

   ☐ Positive reputation and consumer trust.

   ☐ Recognizable brand identity and logo.

2. **Proven Business Model**:

   ☐ Demonstrated success and profitability.

   ☐ Clear guidelines and protocols for operations.

   ☐ Track record of franchisee satisfaction.

3. **Initial Investment Costs**:

    ☐   Initial franchise fee: $ _____

    ☐   Startup costs: (including equipment, inventory, $ _____
    and initial marketing).

    ☐   Additional expenses: (legal fees, training costs, $ _____
    etc.).

4. **Ongoing Fees and Royalties**:

    ☐   Royalty fees: of gross sales.   % _____

    ☐   Advertising fees: of gross sales.   % _____

    ☐   Other ongoing fees: per month/year.   % _____

5. **Support Services Provided by Franchisor**:

    ☐   Initial training program.

    ☐   Ongoing operational support.

    ☐   Marketing and advertising assistance.

    ☐   Technology and software support.

6. **Territory Rights and Restrictions**:

☐   Exclusive territory rights within defined area.

☐   Restrictions on opening additional locations.

☐   Non-compete clauses and territory protection.

7. **Franchise Agreement Terms and Conditions**:

☐   Length of franchise term: _____ years.

☐   Renewal options and conditions.

☐   Termination clauses and exit strategies.

Take Action:

Complete the Franchise Evaluation Checklist for each franchise opportunity you're considering for your business. Use the information gathered to compare and contrast different opportunities and assess their alignment with your business goals and objectives. As you complete the checklist, consider the following question:

Which franchise opportunity best aligns with my long-term vision and objectives for my business, and why?

Use this question as a guide to making informed decisions about franchising and selecting the right opportunity to pursue your entrepreneurial dreams.

Chapter 5

Analyze Your Competition

Key Takeaways

- Identifying Direct and Indirect Competitors

- SWOT Analysis of Competitors

- Activity: Competitor Analysis Worksheet

Welcome to Chapter 5: Analyze Your Competition! As you embark on your journey to establish a successful Party Planning Business, understanding your competitive landscape is crucial. Analyzing your competition not only helps you identify what others are doing well but also reveals gaps in the market that you can capitalize on. This chapter will empower you to gather insights that can inform your strategies and set you apart from the rest.

As a small business owner, it's natural to feel apprehensive about facing established competitors. However, viewing competition as an opportunity rather than a threat can be a game changer. By studying your competitors, you can learn valuable lessons about their strengths and weaknesses, and use this knowledge to refine your own offerings. Remember, competition can drive innovation and motivate you to improve your services.

In this chapter, we will cover:

- Identifying both direct and indirect competitors in the party planning industry.

- Conducting a SWOT analysis to evaluate your competitors' strengths, weaknesses, opportunities, and threats.

- Utilizing the insights gained to develop a competitive edge for your business.

By the end of this chapter, you will have a clearer understanding of where you stand in the marketplace and how you can position your Party Planning Business for success. Embrace this opportunity to learn from others, and let it inspire you to create a unique and compelling service that meets the needs of your target audience. Let's dive in and start analyzing your competition!

Identifying Direct and Indirect Competitors

When starting your own Party Planning Business, understanding your competition is crucial for establishing a successful strategy. Competitors can be categorized into two main types: direct and indirect competitors. Identifying these competitors will help you to position your services effectively in the marketplace.

Direct Competitors are those businesses that offer the same or very similar services as you. They target the same customer base and operate within the same geographic area. For instance, if you plan to provide event planning services for weddings, your direct competitors would include other wedding planners in your locality. They may offer similar packages, pricing, and styles, making them your primary competition.

To identify your direct competitors, consider the following steps:

- Conduct a Google search for party planners in your area. Take note of businesses that appear consistently in search results.

- Check local directories and social media platforms for event planning services. Look for reviews and ratings to gauge their popularity.

- Visit local event venues and ask for their preferred vendor lists. This can provide insight into established planners who frequently work with the venue.

Once you have a list of direct competitors, analyze their strengths and weaknesses. What do they do well? Where do they fall short? This analysis will help you identify gaps in the market that your business can fill.

Indirect Competitors are businesses that offer different services but still compete for the same customer dollar. For example, a catering company might not offer full event planning services but could still attract clients who are looking for a one-stop-shop for their events. Similarly, venues that provide in-house planning services can also be considered indirect competitors.

To identify indirect competitors, consider the following:

- Look for businesses that provide complementary services such as catering, photography, or entertainment. These companies may not directly compete with you but can influence your potential clients' choices.

- Consider businesses that offer DIY options for events, such as rental companies that provide party supplies or decor. These can attract clients who prefer a hands-on approach.

- Research online platforms that connect clients with various service providers, like Thumbtack or Eventective. These platforms may feature a range of services that can indirectly compete with your offerings.

By identifying both direct and indirect competitors, you can develop a comprehensive understanding of the market landscape. This knowledge allows you to differentiate your services by focusing on your unique selling propositions (USPs). For example, if your competitors primarily focus on traditional event planning, you might carve out a niche by specializing in eco-friendly events or themed parties.

In conclusion, recognizing your direct and indirect competitors is a vital step in establishing your Party Planning Business. By analyzing their offerings, strengths, and weaknesses, you can position your services to meet the specific needs of your target audience, ultimately leading to greater success in your venture.

SWOT Analysis of Competitors

Conducting a SWOT analysis of your competitors is a vital step in understanding the competitive landscape of the party planning industry. SWOT stands for Strengths, Weaknesses, Opportunities, and Threats. By analyzing these aspects of your competitors, you can identify areas where you can differentiate your business and capitalize on your competitors' shortcomings.

1. **Strengths:** Begin by identifying the strengths of your competitors. What do they do well? This could include their brand reputation, customer loyalty, unique services, or efficient operations. For example, a competitor may have a strong social media presence that attracts a large audience, or they might offer exclusive party themes that are popular in your area.

   - **Brand Recognition:** A well-known competitor may have established trust and credibility with clients.

   - **Service Offerings:** Look for unique services that set them apart, such as custom party planning or specialized event themes.

   - **Customer Relationships:** Strong relationships can lead to repeat business and referrals.

2. **Weaknesses:** Next, assess your competitors' weaknesses. Where do they fall short? This could involve poor customer service, limited service offerings, or negative reviews. Identifying these weaknesses can help you position your business to fill those gaps.

- **Poor Customer Service:** If a competitor is known for slow response times or unhelpful staff, you can differentiate your business by prioritizing exceptional customer service.

- **Limited Marketing Efforts:** If a competitor is not effectively promoting their services, you can capitalize on this by developing a robust marketing strategy.

- **Niche Market Gaps:** If competitors are not catering to specific demographics or interests (e.g., eco-friendly parties), you can target these underserved markets.

3. **Opportunities:** Look for opportunities that your competitors may not be taking advantage of. This could be emerging trends in the party planning industry, such as virtual events or eco-friendly options. By staying ahead of the curve, you can position your business as a leader in these areas.

- **Emerging Trends:** Consider trends like sustainable events or technology-driven experiences.

- **Market Gaps:** Identify areas where demand exceeds supply, such as themed parties for niche audiences.

- **Partnerships:** Explore potential collaborations with local vendors or venues that your competitors may not have tapped into.

4. **Threats:** Finally, consider the threats your competitors face that might also impact your business. This could include economic downturns, increased competition, or changing consumer preferences. Understanding these threats can help you prepare and develop strategies to mitigate their impact.

    - **Economic Factors:** Economic downturns can reduce overall spending on events, affecting all businesses in the industry.

    - **New Entrants:** Be aware of new competitors entering the market, which can increase competition for clients.

    - **Changing Consumer Preferences:** Trends can shift quickly; staying adaptable is key to responding to these changes.

In conclusion, conducting a SWOT analysis of your competitors provides valuable insights that can guide your business strategy. By understanding their strengths and weaknesses, as well as the opportunities and threats in the market, you can carve out a unique position for your Party Planning Business and increase your chances of success.

Visit **www.BusinessBookstore.com/start** to download blank forms, etc.

Activity: Competitor Analysis Worksheet

Now that you've learned about the importance of analyzing your competitors and conducting a SWOT analysis, it's time to put that knowledge into action. The Competitor Analysis Worksheet provided below will guide you through the process of systematically gathering and organizing information about your competitors. By completing this worksheet, you'll gain valuable insights that inform your competitive strategy and position your business for success.

Instructions:

1. **Identify Your Competitors:** List the main competitors in your industry or market segment. Consider both direct and indirect competitors that may impact your business.

2. **Gather Information:** Research each competitor and gather information about their strengths, weaknesses, opportunities, and threats. Use online resources, industry reports, and customer feedback to gather insights.

3. **Complete the Worksheet:** Fill in the details for each competitor in the appropriate sections of the worksheet. Be thorough and objective in your analysis, focusing on key factors that impact their performance and market position.

4. **Analyze the Results:** Review the completed worksheet to identify trends, patterns, and areas of opportunity or concern. Use this analysis to refine your own competitive strategy and differentiate your business in the market.

Competitor Analysis Worksheet:

Competitor Name:

_____

Strengths:

List the strengths or advantages that the competitor possesses, such as strong brand reputation, innovative products, or extensive market reach.

_____

_____

_____

Weaknesses:

Identify weaknesses or vulnerabilities that may hinder the competitor's success, such as poor customer service, limited product offerings, or financial instability.

_____

_____

_____

Opportunities:

Highlight potential opportunities for growth or innovation that the competitor may be capitalizing on, such as emerging market trends, new customer segments, or technological advancements.

_____

_____

_____

Threats:

Identify threats or challenges that the competitor faces, such as intense competition, regulatory changes, or economic fluctuations.

_____

_____

_____

Conclusion:

Completing the Competitor Analysis Worksheet provides you with a comprehensive understanding of your competitive landscape, enabling you to identify opportunities, mitigate risks, and refine your own competitive strategy. Use the insights gained from this analysis to position your business for success and outperform your competitors in the market.

Chapter 6

Create Your Financial Plan

Key Takeaways

- Estimating Startup Costs

- Projecting Revenue and Expenses

- Activity: Startup Budget Template

Welcome to Chapter 6: Estimate Startup Costs! As you embark on your journey to start your own Party Planning Business, understanding your financial landscape is crucial. Estimating startup costs may seem daunting, but it's an essential step that will empower you to make informed decisions and set your business up for success.

Every successful business begins with a solid financial foundation. By accurately estimating your startup costs, you can not only gauge the initial investment required but also identify potential funding sources and budget effectively for the future. Remember, being prepared financially will help you navigate the challenges that come with launching your business.

In this chapter, we'll explore the various components that contribute to your startup costs, including:

- Equipment and supplies

- Marketing and branding expenses

- Legal fees and permits

- Operational costs such as rent and utilities

We'll also discuss how to project your revenue and expenses, giving you a clearer picture of what to expect as your business grows. This knowledge will not only help you stay organized and focused but also instill confidence in your ability to manage your finances.

As you work through the activities in this chapter, remember that every successful entrepreneur started where you are now. Embrace the process, stay committed to your vision, and take charge of your financial future. Let's dive in and start estimating those startup costs!

Estimating Startup Costs

Estimating startup costs is a crucial step in launching your Party Planning Business. It involves calculating all the expenses you will incur before your business begins to generate revenue. Accurately estimating these costs helps you understand the financial requirements of your business and can guide you in securing funding if needed.

Startup costs can be divided into two main categories: fixed costs and variable costs.

1. **Fixed Costs:** These are expenses that remain constant regardless of your business activity. Examples include:

   - *Business Registration Fees:* This includes the costs associated with registering your business name and entity, which can vary by state or country.

   - *Insurance:* Obtaining business insurance is essential to protect your investment. Research different types of insurance (general liability, professional liability, etc.) and estimate the premiums.

   - *Office Space:* If you plan to rent an office or studio, consider the monthly rent or lease agreement costs. If you work from home, factor in any costs associated with setting up a home office.

   - *Equipment and Supplies:* This includes any furniture, computers, printers, and office supplies you might need to get started.

   - *Website Development:* If you hire a professional to build your website, include those costs. Alternatively, factor in the costs of a domain name and hosting if you plan to create it yourself.

2. **Variable Costs:** These costs fluctuate based on your business activities. Examples include:

- *Marketing and Advertising:* Budget for initial marketing campaigns to promote your services. This could include social media ads, print materials, or local event sponsorships.

- *Supplies for Events:* As a party planner, you will need to purchase supplies for events, such as decorations, catering supplies, and rental items. Estimate these costs based on the types of events you plan to host.

- *Labor Costs:* If you hire staff or freelancers for events, consider their wages. This could include event coordinators, decorators, or catering staff.

- *Transportation:* If you need to travel to events, factor in costs for fuel, vehicle maintenance, or public transportation.

To effectively estimate your startup costs, follow these steps:

- **Create a Detailed List:** Start by listing all potential expenses in both fixed and variable categories. Be as comprehensive as possible.

- **Research Costs:** Use online resources, industry reports, and consultations with other party planners to gather accurate cost estimates for each item on your list.

- **Consult with Professionals:** If you're unsure about specific costs, consider consulting with an accountant or financial advisor who understands small business startups.

- **Prepare for Contingencies:** It's wise to include a buffer of 10-20% of your total estimated costs to account for unexpected expenses that may arise.

Once you have compiled and estimated your startup costs, review them to ensure they align with your financial goals and available resources. This will give you a clearer picture of the funding you may need to secure and help you make informed decisions as you embark on your party planning venture.

Projecting Revenue and Expenses

Projecting revenue and expenses is a crucial step in estimating the financial viability of your Party Planning Business. This process involves forecasting your expected income and expenses over a specific period, usually the first year, to help you understand your cash flow and make informed decisions. Here's how to approach this task effectively.

1. **Estimating Revenue**: Your revenue projections should be based on realistic expectations of how much business you anticipate generating. Start by considering the following:

    *   **Service Offerings:** List the various services you will offer, such as event planning, coordination, decoration, and catering. Consider any packages or add-ons you might provide.

    *   **Pricing Strategy:** Determine how much you will charge for each service. Research competitors to find a competitive yet profitable pricing structure.

    *   **Expected Client Volume:** Estimate the number of clients you expect to serve each month. This could be based on market research or industry averages.

For example, if you plan to offer three different packages priced at $1,000, $2,000, and $3,000, and you expect to sell 2 of each per month, your projected monthly revenue would be:

*   (2 x $1,000) + (2 x $2,000) + (2 x $3,000) = $2,000 + $4,000 + $6,000 = $12,000

2. **Estimating Expenses**: Next, you need to identify your expected expenses. These can be divided into fixed and variable costs:

- **Fixed Costs:** These are expenses that do not change regardless of how many clients you have. Examples include:

  - Rent for your office or storage space

  - Insurance premiums

  - Salaries for any employees or contractors

- **Variable Costs:** These costs fluctuate based on the volume of business. Examples include:

  - Supplies and materials for events (decorations, catering, etc.)

  - Marketing and advertising expenses

  - Transportation costs for delivering services

For instance, if your fixed costs total $3,000 per month and your variable costs average $2,000 per event, and you expect to handle 4 events a month, your total expenses would be:

- **Fixed Costs:** $3,000

- **Variable Costs:** 4 x $2,000 = $8,000

- **Total Expenses:** $3,000 + $8,000 = $11,000

3. **Calculating Profit**: Once you have your revenue and expenses projected, you can calculate your expected profit:

- **Projected Revenue:** $12,000

- **Projected Expenses:** $11,000

- **Projected Profit:** $12,000 - $11,000 = $1,000

This projection indicates you would make a profit of $1,000 in your first month, which is a positive sign for your business's sustainability.

4. **Adjusting Your Projections**: Keep in mind that these projections should be revisited regularly. As you gain experience and data from your operations, you may need to adjust your revenue estimates, refine your pricing, or manage expenses more effectively. Utilize accounting software or spreadsheets to track your actual income and expenses against your projections for better insights.

By carefully projecting your revenue and expenses, you can create a financial roadmap for your Party Planning Business that will guide you toward achieving your goals.

Visit **www.BusinessBookstore.com/start** to download blank forms, etc.

Activity: Startup Budget Template

As you've learned, creating a comprehensive financial plan is essential for the success and sustainability of your business. The Startup Budget Template provided below will serve as a practical tool to help you organize and plan your startup expenses, revenue projections, and overall financial outlook.

Instructions:

1. **Fill in each section:** Use the knowledge and insights gained from previous chapters to fill in each section of the Startup Budget Template with relevant information about your business.

2. **Be detailed and realistic:** Provide detailed estimates for startup expenses and revenue projections, taking into account factors such as market research, industry trends, and business assumptions.

3. **Regularly update and review:** As your business evolves, regularly update and review your startup budget to reflect changes in expenses, revenue, and overall financial performance.

Startup Budget Template:

INITIAL EXPENSES:

Business registration and legal fees: $ _____

Lease or rental deposit: $ _____

Utility setup fees: $ _____

Initial inventory purchases: $ _____

Store signage and branding: $ _____

Technology and POS system setup: $ _____

Furniture and fixtures: $ _____

Initial marketing and advertising: $ _____

Professional services (legal, accounting, etc.): $ _____

Miscellaneous expenses: $ _____

TOTAL Initial Expenses: $ _____

ONGOING MONTHLY EXPENSES:

Rent or lease payments: $ _____

Utilities (electricity, water, internet, etc.): $ _____

Inventory purchases and restocking: $ _____

Employee salaries and wages: $ _____

Marketing and advertising costs: $ _____

Insurance (business liability, property, etc.): $ _____

Equipment maintenance and repairs: $ _____

Professional services (accounting, legal, etc.): $ _____

Loan repayments (if applicable): $ _____

Miscellaneous expenses: $ _____

TOTAL Monthly Expenses: $ _____

Estimated monthly sales: $ _____

FUNDING SOURCES:

Personal savings: $ _____

Small business loan: $ _____

Investment from partners or investors: $ _____

Grants or government funding: $ _____

Crowdfunding or peer-to-peer lending: $ _____

Other sources: $ _____

TOTAL Funding: $ _____

Conclusion:

Completing the Startup Budget Template provides you with a clear and organized view of your business's financial outlook, enabling you to make informed decisions and navigate the financial challenges of entrepreneurship with confidence. Use this tool as a guiding framework for managing your startup finances and driving success in your business.

Chapter 7

Choose Your Legal Structure

Key Takeaways

- Understanding Different Legal Structures

- Registering Your Business Entity

- Activity: Legal Structure Comparison Checklist

As you embark on the exciting journey of starting your own Party Planning Business, one crucial step is to choose the right legal structure. This decision not only impacts your business operations but also influences your liability, tax obligations, and ability to raise capital. Understanding the various legal structures available can empower you to make an informed choice that aligns with your goals and vision.

Choosing the appropriate legal structure is essential for protecting your personal assets and ensuring compliance with local regulations. Whether you opt for a sole proprietorship, partnership, limited liability company (LLC), or corporation, each structure comes with its own set of advantages and challenges. By familiarizing yourself with these options, you can select the one that best suits your business model and long-term aspirations.

In this chapter, we will explore:

- **Understanding Different Legal Structures:** Learn about the various legal entities available and their implications for your business.

- **Registering Your Business Entity:** Discover the steps involved in officially establishing your business and ensuring it operates within the law.

Remember, this is a significant milestone in your entrepreneurial journey. By taking the time to understand and choose the right legal structure, you are laying a strong foundation for your business's future success. Embrace this opportunity to protect your vision and ensure that your hard work pays off. Let's dive in and equip you with the knowledge you need to make this important decision confidently!

Understanding Different Legal Structures

When starting your own Party Planning Business, one of the crucial decisions you will face is choosing the right legal structure for your company. The legal structure you select will impact your taxes, liability, and the overall management of your business. Here's an overview of the most common legal structures you might consider:

- **Sole Proprietorship:** This is the simplest and most common structure for small businesses. As a sole proprietor, you are the sole owner and operator of the business. You have complete control over all decisions and keep all profits, but you are also personally liable for any debts or legal issues that arise. This means that your personal assets could be at risk if your business faces financial trouble.

- **Partnership:** If you plan to start your business with one or more partners, a partnership may be the right choice. In a partnership, two or more individuals share ownership and responsibilities. There are different types of partnerships, including general partnerships, where all partners are equally responsible, and limited partnerships, where some partners have limited liability. It's essential to draft a partnership agreement that outlines each partner's roles, responsibilities, and profit-sharing arrangements.

- **Limited Liability Company (LLC):** An LLC combines the benefits of a sole proprietorship and a corporation. It provides personal liability protection to its owners, known as members, meaning that personal assets are generally protected from business debts and lawsuits. Additionally, LLCs offer flexibility in management and taxation. Profits and losses can be passed through to members' personal tax returns, avoiding double taxation. This structure is popular among small business owners due to its simplicity and protection.

- **Corporation:** A corporation is a more complex legal structure that separates the business from its owners. It can be beneficial for larger businesses or those seeking to raise capital through investors. Corporations offer limited liability protection, meaning owners are not personally liable for business debts. However, corporations face more regulations and higher costs to establish and maintain. There are different types of corporations, including C-corporations and S-corporations, each with distinct tax implications.

When deciding which legal structure is best for your Party Planning Business, consider the following factors:

- **Liability:** How much personal liability are you willing to assume? If you want to protect your personal assets, an LLC or corporation may be the better choice.

- **Taxes:** Different structures have varying tax implications. Consult with a tax professional to understand how each structure will affect your taxes.

- **Control:** Do you want to maintain full control over your business decisions, or are you open to sharing control with partners?

- **Costs:** Consider the costs associated with setting up and maintaining each legal structure. Some may require more paperwork and fees than others.

In conclusion, understanding the different legal structures available for your Party Planning Business is essential for making informed decisions. Each option has its advantages and disadvantages, so take the time to evaluate what aligns best with your business goals and personal circumstances. Consulting with a legal professional can also provide valuable insights tailored to your specific situation.

Registering Your Business Entity

Registering your business entity is a crucial step in establishing your Party Planning Business. This process not only legitimizes your business but also protects your personal assets and provides various benefits, such as tax advantages and credibility with clients. Here, we will explore the different types of business structures, the registration process, and essential considerations to keep in mind.

There are several common types of business structures you can choose from:

- **Sole Proprietorship:** This is the simplest form of business entity, where you are the sole owner and responsible for all aspects of the business. While it is easy to set up, it does not provide personal liability protection.

- **Partnership:** If you plan to start your business with one or more partners, a partnership may be the right choice. In a partnership, all partners share profits, losses, and responsibilities. However, like sole proprietorships, partners may be personally liable for business debts.

- **Limited Liability Company (LLC):** An LLC combines the benefits of a corporation and a sole proprietorship/partnership. It provides personal liability protection while allowing for flexible management and tax treatment. This is a popular choice for small business owners.

- **Corporation:** A corporation is a more complex business structure that is legally separate from its owners. It offers the strongest protection against personal liability but involves more regulatory requirements and tax obligations.

Once you have decided on the business structure that best fits your needs, the next step is to register your business entity. Here's how to do it:

1. **Choose a Business Name:** Your business name should reflect your brand and be unique. Make sure it complies with your state's naming requirements and is not already in use by another business.

2. **Check Name Availability:** Before registering, check if your desired business name is available. You can do this through your state's business registration website or by searching online databases.

3. **File the Necessary Documents:** Depending on your chosen business structure, you will need to file specific documents with your state. For example:

    *   For an LLC, you will typically file Articles of Organization.

    *   For a corporation, you will need to file Articles of Incorporation.

4. **Pay the Registration Fees:** Each state has different fees associated with registering a business entity. Be prepared to pay these fees during the registration process.

5. **Obtain an Employer Identification Number (EIN):** After registering your business entity, apply for an EIN from the IRS. This number is essential for tax purposes and will be necessary if you plan to hire employees.

Keep in mind that requirements may vary by state, so it is essential to research your specific state's regulations and procedures. Additionally, consider consulting with a legal professional or a business advisor to ensure you are making the best decisions for your business.

In summary, registering your business entity is a vital step in launching your Party Planning Business. By selecting the right business structure and following the registration process, you will lay a strong foundation for your business's success.

Visit **www.BusinessBookstore.com/start** to register your business.

Activity: Legal Structure Comparison Checklist

The Legal Structure Comparison Checklist provided below will assist you in evaluating and comparing different legal structures for your business. By completing this checklist, you'll gain clarity on the advantages, disadvantages, and suitability of each structure based on your specific needs and circumstances.

Instructions:

- **Review Each Legal Structure:** Familiarize yourself with the characteristics and implications of sole proprietorships, partnerships, limited liability companies (LLCs), and corporations as discussed previously.

- **Evaluate Based on Your Business Needs:** Consider factors such as liability protection, taxation, management flexibility, and regulatory requirements when assessing each legal structure.

- **Complete the Checklist:** For each legal structure, indicate whether it aligns with your business goals and preferences by checking the corresponding boxes.

- **Consider Professional Advice:** Consult with legal and financial professionals to further assess your options and make an informed decision about the most suitable legal structure for your business.

Legal Structure Comparison Checklist:

Criteria	Sole Proprietorship	Partnership	LLC	Corporation
Liability Protection				
Taxation				
Management Flexibility				
Regulatory Requirements				
Ease of Formation				
Ownership Structure				
Continuity of Existence				
Cost of Formation and Maintenance				
Tax Reporting Requirements				

Conclusion:

Completing the Legal Structure Comparison Checklist will provide you with valuable insights into the suitability of each legal structure for your business. Use this tool as a guiding framework to make an informed decision that aligns with your business goals and aspirations.

Chapter 8

Draft Your Business Plan

Key Takeaways

- Executive Summary and Company Description

- Market Analysis and Marketing Strategy

- Activity: Business Plan Outline Template

Welcome to Chapter 8: Draft Your Business Plan! As you embark on the journey of starting your own Party Planning Business, creating a solid business plan is one of the most crucial steps you can take. A well-structured business plan serves as a roadmap, guiding you through the various phases of your business and helping you stay focused on your goals.

Many aspiring entrepreneurs may feel overwhelmed at the thought of drafting a business plan, but remember, this document is not just a formality; it is an opportunity to clarify your vision, define your objectives, and outline the strategies that will lead to your success. Think of it as a dynamic tool that will evolve alongside your business, adapting to new challenges and opportunities.

Your business plan will encompass key elements such as:

- **Executive Summary:** A brief overview of your business concept and goals.

- **Market Analysis:** Insights into your target market and competitive landscape.

- **Marketing Strategy:** How you plan to reach and engage your audience.

- **Financial Projections:** Estimates of your revenue, expenses, and profitability.

By taking the time to thoughtfully draft your business plan, you will not only gain a deeper understanding of your business model but also build confidence in your ability to execute your vision. This chapter will provide you with the tools and templates necessary to create a comprehensive business plan that reflects your unique aspirations and sets you on the path to success. Let's get started!

Executive Summary and Company Description

The Executive Summary and Company Description are critical components of your business plan. They provide a snapshot of your business, its mission, and the strategies you will employ to achieve your goals. This section should be concise yet comprehensive, allowing readers to quickly grasp the essence of your Party Planning Business.

Executive Summary

The Executive Summary serves as an overview of your entire business plan. It should summarize the key points that will be elaborated on in the subsequent sections. Here are some essential elements to include:

- **Business Name and Location:** Clearly state the name of your Party Planning Business and its physical or virtual location. For example, "Celebration Creations, based in Austin, Texas."

- **Business Concept:** Describe what your business does. For instance, "Celebration Creations specializes in planning and executing memorable events such as weddings, corporate functions, and birthday parties."

- **Target Market:** Identify who your ideal customers are. You might say, "Our target market includes busy professionals, engaged couples, and families looking to celebrate milestones in a stress-free manner."

- **Unique Selling Proposition (USP):** Highlight what sets your business apart from competitors. For example, "We offer personalized event planning services that cater to individual preferences, ensuring each event is uniquely tailored to our clients' needs."

- **Financial Projections:** Provide a brief overview of your financial outlook. You could include, "We project a revenue of $100,000 in our first year, with a growth rate of 20% annually as we expand our client base."

Company Description

The Company Description section provides more in-depth information about your business. This is where you can elaborate on your mission, vision, and the values that guide your operations. Consider the following components:

- **Mission Statement:** Craft a clear and compelling mission statement that defines your business's purpose. For instance, "At Celebration Creations, our mission is to transform our clients' visions into unforgettable experiences through meticulous planning and exceptional service."

- **Vision Statement:** Outline the long-term goals and aspirations of your business. An example could be, "We envision becoming the leading party planning service in Texas, known for our innovative ideas and outstanding customer satisfaction."

- **Core Values:** Identify the principles that guide your business decisions. Examples might include integrity, creativity, customer focus, and teamwork.

- **Business Structure:** Specify the legal structure of your business (e.g., sole proprietorship, LLC, corporation) and explain why you chose this structure. For example, "Celebration Creations is registered as an LLC to protect personal assets and provide flexibility in management."

- **History and Background:** If applicable, provide a brief history of how and why you started your business. You might mention, "Founded in 2023, Celebration Creations was born from a passion for event planning and a desire to help others celebrate life's special moments."

In summary, the Executive Summary and Company Description are foundational elements of your business plan. They should clearly communicate your business's purpose, goals, and unique attributes to potential investors, partners, and clients. Take the time to craft these sections thoughtfully, as they will set the stage for the rest of your business plan.

Market Analysis and Marketing Strategy

Conducting a thorough market analysis and developing a robust marketing strategy are critical steps in creating a successful Party Planning Business. Understanding the market landscape allows you to identify opportunities, anticipate challenges, and tailor your services to meet customer needs effectively.

Market Analysis

Market analysis involves examining various factors that influence your business environment. Here are some key components to consider:

- **Industry Trends:** Stay informed about the latest trends in the party planning industry. For instance, eco-friendly events and personalized experiences are gaining popularity. Research industry reports and attend trade shows to gather insights.

- **Competitive Landscape:** Analyze your competitors by identifying their strengths and weaknesses. Look at their service offerings, pricing, and customer feedback. This information will help you differentiate your business and find your unique selling proposition (USP).

- **Market Size and Growth:** Estimate the size of your target market and its growth potential. Use demographic data and market research reports to understand how many potential clients you can reach.

Marketing Strategy

Once you have completed your market analysis, you can develop a marketing strategy that aligns with your business goals. Here are some essential elements to include:

1. **Target Market Identification:** Define your target audience based on demographics, interests, and behaviors. For example, if you specialize in children's parties, your target market may include parents aged 25-40 who value memorable experiences for their children.

2. **Value Proposition:** Clearly articulate what sets your party planning services apart. Whether it's your attention to detail, creativity, or exceptional customer service, make sure your value proposition resonates with your target audience.

3. **Marketing Channels:** Choose the most effective channels to reach your target audience. Consider a mix of online and offline strategies, such as:

   - *Social Media:* Utilize platforms like Instagram and Pinterest to showcase your event designs and engage with potential clients.

   - *Email Marketing:* Build an email list to send newsletters, promotions, and updates about your services.

   - *Networking Events:* Attend local business events to connect with potential clients and other vendors in the industry.

4. **Budgeting for Marketing:** Allocate a budget for your marketing efforts. Track your expenses and evaluate the return on investment (ROI) for each marketing channel to ensure effective spending.

As you implement your marketing strategy, continuously monitor its effectiveness and be prepared to make adjustments as needed. Collect feedback from clients and keep an eye on industry trends to stay relevant and competitive.

In summary, a comprehensive market analysis combined with a well-defined marketing strategy will position your Party Planning Business for success. By understanding your market and effectively promoting your services, you can attract and retain clients, ultimately leading to a thriving business.

Visit **www.BusinessBookstore.com/start** to download blank forms, etc.

Activity: Business Plan Outline Template

Now it's time to put all the insights and strategies you've learned into action by drafting your own business plan. Below is a comprehensive Business Plan Outline Template to guide you through the process. By filling out each section of the template, you'll create a structured roadmap for your business's success.

Instructions:

1. **Review Each Section:** Familiarize yourself with the components of the Business Plan Outline Template, including Executive Summary, Company Description, Market Analysis, Marketing Strategy, Financial Plan, and more.

2. **Fill Out Each Section:** For each section, provide detailed information about your business concept, target market, competitive landscape, marketing strategies, financial projections, and operational plans. Use the insights and strategies discussed in this chapter to inform your responses.

3. **Be Clear and Concise:** Keep your responses clear, concise, and focused on key points. Highlight the unique aspects of your business and articulate your vision, goals, and strategies effectively.

4. **Seek Feedback:** Once you've completed the template, seek feedback from mentors, advisors, or peers to ensure your business plan is thorough, coherent, and compelling.

Business Plan Outline Template:

1. **Executive Summary:**

- Overview of your business concept, mission, and objectives.

  _____

  _____

  _____

- Summary of key components of the business plan.

  _____

  _____

  _____

- Highlight of your unique value proposition and competitive advantage.

  _____

  _____

  _____

2. **Company Description:**

- History, vision, and core values of your business.

  _____

  _____

  _____

- Description of products or services offered.

  _____

  _____

  _____

- Target market segments and customer demographics.

  _____

  _____

  _____

- Competitive analysis and positioning in the market.

  _____

  _____

  _____

3. **Market Analysis:**

- Analysis of industry trends and market dynamics.

  _____

  _____

  _____

- Segmentation of target market and customer personas.

  _____

  _____

  _____

- Competitive landscape and SWOT analysis.

  _____

  _____

  _____

- Customer insights and needs assessment.

  _____

  _____

  _____

4. Marketing Strategy:

- Value proposition and unique selling proposition (USP).

  _____

  _____

  _____

- Selection of marketing channels and tactics.

  _____

  _____

  _____

- Content and messaging strategy.

  _____

  _____

  _____

- Marketing goals and KPIs.

  _____

  _____

  _____

5. **Financial Plan:**

- Startup costs and funding requirements.

_____

_____

_____

- Revenue projections and sales forecasts.

_____

_____

Operating expenses and cost structure.

_____

_____

_____

- Cash flow projections and break-even analysis.

_____

_____

_____

6. **Operational Plan:**

• Organizational structure and management team.

_____

_____

_____

• Production or service delivery processes.

_____

_____

_____

• Technology requirements and infrastructure.

_____

_____

_____

• Suppliers, vendors, and distribution channels.

_____

_____

_____

7. **Appendices:**

- Additional documents, research findings, or supporting materials.

_____

_____

_____

Conclusion:

Completing the Business Plan Outline Template will provide you with a structured framework for organizing your ideas and strategies into a comprehensive business plan. Use this template as a guiding tool to articulate your vision, set goals and create a roadmap for success. Good luck on your entrepreneurial journey!

Start Your Business

Chapter 9

Register Your Business Name

Key Takeaways

- Checking Name Availability and Reserving Domain

- Filing Legal Documentation

- Activity: Business Name Availability Check Form

Welcome to Chapter 9: **Register Your Business Name**. As you embark on the exciting journey of launching your own Party Planning Business, one of the most crucial steps you'll take is selecting and registering your business name. This name will not only represent your brand but also create a lasting impression on your clients. It's your first opportunity to showcase your creativity and professionalism, so take this step seriously!

Choosing the right name is essential for establishing your identity in the competitive world of event planning. A well-thought-out business name can help you stand out, attract your target audience, and convey the essence of your services. Remember, your business name is often the first thing potential clients will see, so it should resonate with them and reflect what you offer.

In this chapter, we will guide you through the process of checking name availability, reserving a domain, and filing the necessary legal documentation to secure your business name. Here's what you can expect:

- **Checking Name Availability:** Learn how to ensure your chosen name isn't already in use.

- **Reserving Your Domain:** Understand the importance of having a matching online presence.

- **Filing Legal Documentation:** Get familiar with the steps to officially register your business name.

By the end of this chapter, you will have a clear understanding of how to select and secure a name that will serve as the foundation of your brand. So, let's dive in and take this important step towards building a successful Party Planning Business!

Checking Name Availability and Reserving Domain

Choosing the right name for your Party Planning Business is a crucial step in establishing your brand identity. A well-thought-out name can convey your services, attract your target audience, and set you apart from competitors. However, before you settle on a name, it's essential to check its availability and secure a domain name for your online presence.

1. **Checking Name Availability**: The first step in ensuring your business name is viable is to check its availability. Here are some methods to do this:

   - **Search Online:** Start by conducting a simple online search using search engines. Type in your desired business name and see if any existing businesses are using it. Look for similar names that could cause confusion.

   - **Social Media Platforms:** Check major social media platforms like Facebook, Instagram, and Twitter/X to see if the name is already in use. Consistent branding across platforms is important, so aim for the same name wherever possible.

   - **Business Name Registries:** Visit your local or state business registry website. Most jurisdictions maintain a database of registered business names, allowing you to see if your desired name is already taken.

   - **Trademark Search:** Conduct a trademark search through the United States Patent and Trademark Office (USPTO) or your country's trademark office. This will help you determine if your name is trademarked by another entity, which could lead to legal issues down the line.

2. **Reserving Your Business Name**: Once you've confirmed that your chosen name is available, you can reserve it. Many states allow you to reserve a business name for a specific period, usually ranging from 30 to 120 days. This can be done through the state's business registration office, often for a small fee. Reserving your name is a smart move if you need more time to finalize your business plans.

3. **Securing Your Domain Name**: In today's digital age, having an online presence is vital for any business. Securing a domain name that matches your business name is an important step:

   • **Domain Name Registrars:** Use domain registrars such as BusinessBookstore.com, GoDaddy, Namecheap, or Google Domains to search for your desired domain name. Ideally, your domain should be as close to your business name as possible.

   • **Consider Variations:** If your preferred domain is unavailable, consider variations. For instance, if **yourbusinessname.com** is taken, you might try **yourbusinessnameonline.com** or **yourbusinessnameevents.com**.

   • **Domain Extensions:** While .com is the most recognized domain extension, don't hesitate to explore others like .net, .co, or industry-specific extensions such as .events or .party.

4. **Registering Your Domain**: Once you find an available domain name, register it immediately. Domain names can be snatched up quickly, so acting fast is crucial. Registration typically involves an annual fee, and many registrars offer additional services like domain privacy protection to keep your personal information private.

In summary, checking name availability and reserving a domain are foundational steps in launching your Party Planning Business. A unique name and a matching online presence will help you establish credibility and attract clients. Take the time to research thoroughly and secure your business identity effectively.

Filing Legal Documentation

Once you have chosen a business name and ensured its availability, the next crucial step in establishing your Party Planning Business is to file the necessary legal documentation. This process can vary depending on your location and the legal structure you choose for your business. Below are the key steps you should follow to ensure that your business is legally registered and compliant with local regulations.

1. **Choose Your Business Structure**: Your business structure will determine the type of legal documentation you need to file. Common structures include:

   - **Sole Proprietorship:** This is the simplest structure, requiring minimal paperwork. You may need to file a "Doing Business As" (DBA) If your business name differs from your legal name.

   - **Partnership:** Similar to sole proprietorships, partnerships may require a DBA. Additionally, a partnership agreement outlining the roles and responsibilities of each partner is advisable.

   - **Limited Liability Company (LLC):** Filing Articles of Organization with your state is necessary for LLCs. This document outlines the basic details of your business and its members.

   - **Corporation:** Corporations must file Articles of Incorporation, which include information about the corporation's structure, purpose, and stock details.

2. **Register Your Business Name**: After determining your business structure, you will need to officially register your business name. This step typically involves:

    - Checking name availability through your state's business registry.

    - Filing the necessary documentation, such as a DBA registration if applicable.

    - Considering trademark registration if your brand name is unique and you wish to protect it legally.

3. **Obtain an Employer Identification Number (EIN)**: If you plan to hire employees or operate as a corporation or partnership, you will need to apply for an Employer Identification Number (EIN) from the Internal Revenue Service (IRS). This number is essential for tax purposes and can be obtained easily online through the IRS website.

4. **File for Necessary Permits and Licenses**: Depending on your location and the nature of your Party Planning Business, you may need specific permits or licenses. Common examples include:

    - **Business License:** Most cities require a general business license to operate legally.

    - **Sales Tax Permit:** If you plan to sell products or services that are taxable, you will need to apply for a sales tax permit.

    - **Special Event Permits:** If you are organizing events in public spaces, check with local authorities for any required permits.

5. **Keep Records of All Documentation**: Once you have filed your legal documentation, it's crucial to keep organized records. Maintain copies of all filed documents, correspondence with government agencies, and any permits or licenses you obtain. This organization will help you manage your business effectively and prepare for any future legal or financial audits.

By following these steps and ensuring that all legal documentation is properly filed, you will lay a strong foundation for your Party Planning Business. This process may seem complex, but taking it step by step will help you navigate the legal landscape with confidence.

Visit **www.BusinessBookstore.com/start** to register your business.

Activity: Business Name Availability Check Form

Before finalizing your business name, it's crucial to ensure that it's available for use and doesn't infringe on existing trademarks or business entities. Use the following form to conduct a thorough check of your desired business name's availability:

Business Name Availability Check Form

1. **Proposed Business Name:**_____

2. **Business Structure:** Select the business structure you're considering: Sole Proprietorship / Partnership / Limited Liability Company (LLC) / Corporation

3. **Check State Business Registry:**

   ☐ Search the online database of your state's business registry to see if the proposed name is already registered by another business entity.
   ☐ Note any similar or identical names that may pose potential conflicts.

4. **Search U.S. Patent and Trademark Office (USPTO) Database:**

   ☐ Visit the USPTO website and conduct a trademark search to determine if the proposed name is already trademarked.
   ☐ Pay attention to any existing trademarks that may overlap with your proposed business name.

5. **Domain Name Availability:**

☐ Check the availability of the corresponding domain name for your business.

☐ Search domain registration websites to see if your desired domain name is available for purchase.

6. **Additional Considerations:**

☐ Consider the availability of social media handles associated with your proposed business name.

☐ Evaluate the overall availability and uniqueness of the name in your industry and market.

7. **Final Decision:**

☐ Based on the results of your research, determine if the proposed business name is available for use.

☐ If the name is available, proceed with registering it for your business. If not, brainstorm alternative names and repeat the availability check process.

Instructions: Complete each section of the form by performing the specified actions. Be thorough in your research to ensure that your chosen business name is available and legally sound. Once you've completed the form and confirmed the availability of your desired name, you can proceed with confidence in establishing your business identity.

Chapter 10

Obtain Necessary Business Licenses and Permits

Key Takeaways

- Researching Local Regulations and Requirements

- Applying for Licenses and Permits

- Activity: Licenses and Permits Checklist

As you embark on the exciting journey of starting your own Party Planning Business, one of the critical steps you'll need to navigate is obtaining the necessary licenses and permits. While this process might seem daunting at first, it is an essential part of establishing a legitimate and successful business. Securing the right licenses not only helps you comply with local laws but also enhances your credibility in the eyes of clients and vendors.

Every region has its own regulations regarding business operations, and understanding these requirements is vital. By taking the time to research and gather the necessary documentation, you can set a strong foundation for your business. Remember, the effort you put into this process will pay off in the long run, allowing you to focus on what you do best—creating unforgettable events for your clients.

In this chapter, we will guide you through:

- Researching local regulations and requirements that pertain to your business.

- Applying for the appropriate licenses and permits.

- Understanding the importance of compliance and how it can benefit your business.

As you work through the activities in this chapter, stay positive and proactive. Each step you take brings you closer to realizing your dream of owning a successful Party Planning Business. Remember, every great achievement begins with the decision to try. Let's get started!

Researching Local Regulations and Requirements

Starting a Party Planning Business involves more than just creativity and organizational skills; it also requires a thorough understanding of the local regulations and requirements that govern your operations. This knowledge is critical to ensure compliance and to avoid potential legal issues that could jeopardize your business. In this section, we will explore key areas you need to research to successfully navigate the regulatory landscape.

1. **Business Licenses:** Almost every business needs a license to operate legally. The type of license you'll require can vary based on your location and the services you provide. For instance, if you plan to host events that include food and beverages, you might need a catering license or a permit to serve alcohol. Check with your local city or county clerk's office to determine the specific licenses required for your Party Planning Business.

2. **Permits:** In addition to business licenses, various permits may be necessary, especially if you are organizing events in public spaces. Here are some common permits you might need:

   - **Event Permits:** Required for hosting events in public parks or venues.

   - **Noise Permits:** May be needed if your event involves loud music or entertainment.

   - **Temporary Structure Permits:** If you plan to set up tents, stages, or other structures, you may need a permit.

Contact your local government's zoning and planning department to inquire about the specific permits applicable to your events.

3. **Health and Safety Regulations:** Depending on the scale and nature of your events, you may need to comply with health and safety regulations. For example, if you are providing food, you must adhere to food safety standards set by your local health department. This may require obtaining a food handler's permit or having your catering service licensed. Familiarize yourself with the health codes in your area to ensure that your events meet all safety standards.

4. **Insurance Requirements:** While not a regulatory requirement in every case, obtaining business insurance is highly recommended. It protects you from liabilities that could arise during events, such as accidents or property damage. Research the types of insurance available, such as general liability insurance, professional liability insurance, and event cancellation insurance, and determine which policies are necessary for your business model.

5. **Zoning Laws:** Zoning laws dictate where you can operate your business and host events. Certain areas may have restrictions on commercial activities, noise levels, and the types of events that can be held. It is essential to check local zoning regulations to ensure that your planned activities comply with the law. This can usually be done through your local zoning office or building department.

6. **Employment Regulations:** If you plan to hire staff for your events, familiarize yourself with local employment laws. This includes understanding wage laws, worker's compensation requirements, and any necessary employee permits. Ensure you are compliant with regulations regarding hiring practices, employee rights, and workplace safety.

In summary, researching local regulations and requirements is a crucial step in establishing your Party Planning Business. By taking the time to understand the necessary licenses, permits, health and safety regulations, insurance needs, zoning laws, and employment regulations, you will lay a solid foundation for your business and minimize the risk of legal complications in the future. Remember to consult with legal professionals or local business advisors if you have specific questions or need assistance navigating these regulations.

Applying for Licenses and Permits

Once you have a clear understanding of the local regulations and requirements for starting a Party Planning Business, the next step is to apply for the necessary licenses and permits. This process can vary significantly depending on your location, the nature of your services, and any specific local regulations. Here's a step-by-step guide to help you navigate this important phase of your business setup.

1. **Research Local Regulations**: Before applying for any licenses or permits, it's crucial to conduct thorough research on the regulations that apply to your business. Start by checking with your local government or business licensing office. Here are some key areas to investigate:

    - **Business License:** Most cities require a general business license to operate legally. This license legitimizes your business and may need to be renewed annually.

    - **Special Permits:** Depending on the services you offer, you may need additional permits. For example, if you plan to serve alcohol at events, you will need a liquor license.

    - **Health and Safety Regulations:** If your services involve food preparation or handling, you may need health permits and to comply with food safety regulations.

    - **Zoning Laws:** Ensure that your business location complies with zoning laws that dictate what types of businesses can operate in specific areas.

2. **Prepare Required Documentation**: Once you have identified the licenses and permits you need, gather the necessary documentation to support your applications. Common documents may include:

   • Proof of identity and business ownership (e.g., tax ID number, articles of incorporation)

   • Proof of insurance (if required)

   • Detailed descriptions of your services and business operations

   • Any additional documentation specific to the permits you are applying for (e.g., health inspection certificates)

3. **Complete the Application Process**: With your documentation ready, you can begin the application process. Here are some tips:

   • **Fill Out Applications Accurately:** Ensure that all information provided on the application forms is accurate and complete to avoid delays.

   • **Understand Fees:** Be prepared to pay application fees for each license or permit. Fees can vary widely, so check your local government's website for specific amounts.

   • **Submit Applications:** Some licenses can be applied for online, while others may require in-person submissions. Follow the instructions carefully for each application.

4. **Follow Up on Applications**: After submitting your applications, it's important to follow up to ensure they are being processed. Here's how:

   • Keep a record of submission dates and any tracking numbers provided.

   • Contact the licensing authority if you haven't received a response within the expected timeframe.

   • Be prepared to provide additional information or clarification if requested by the licensing office.

5. **Maintain Compliance**: Once you have obtained the necessary licenses and permits, ensure that you maintain compliance with all regulations. This includes:

   • Renewing licenses and permits as required.

   • Staying informed about any changes in local laws that may affect your business.

   • Keeping all documentation organized and accessible for inspections or audits.

Applying for licenses and permits can be a time-consuming process, but it is essential for operating your Party Planning Business legally and successfully. Taking the time to understand and fulfill these requirements will help you build a solid foundation for your business.

Visit **www.BusinessBookstore.com/start** to download blank forms, etc.

Activity: Licenses and Permits Checklist

Before launching your business, it's essential to ensure that you have obtained all the necessary licenses and permits required to operate legally. Use the checklist below to track your progress and ensure compliance with regulatory requirements.

Remember to check with your local government offices or regulatory agencies to confirm the specific licenses and permits applicable to your business. Stay organized and proactive in fulfilling these requirements to avoid delays or penalties.

Once you have completed each item on this checklist, you can proceed with confidence, knowing that your business is compliant with all necessary licenses and permits.

This checklist serves as a comprehensive guide to help you navigate the process of obtaining licenses and permits for your business. By diligently completing each item, you're taking important steps towards ensuring legal compliance and operational readiness.

Licenses and Permits Checklist

☐ **Business Registration:** Register your business with the appropriate government authorities (e.g., state, county, city).

☐ **Professional Licenses:** Obtain any professional licenses required for your industry or profession (e.g., medical, legal, cosmetology).

☐ **Zoning Permits:** Check and obtain zoning permits to ensure your business location complies with local zoning regulations.

☐ **Health Department Permits:** Obtain health department permits if your business involves food handling, preparation, or serving.

☐ **Sales Tax Permit:** Apply for a sales tax permit if you will be selling goods or services subject to sales tax.

☐ **Alcohol and Tobacco Permits:** If applicable, obtain permits for selling alcohol or tobacco products.

☐ **Environmental Permits:** Obtain any necessary environmental permits if your business operations may impact the environment.

☐ **Building Permits:** Obtain building permits for any construction, renovations, or alterations to your business premises.

☐ **Signage Permits:** If installing signage, obtain permits from the local authorities as required.

☐ **Fire Department Permits:** Obtain permits related to fire safety and prevention for your business premises.

☐ **Occupational Safety and Health Administration (OSHA) Compliance:** Ensure compliance with OSHA regulations relevant to your industry and workplace safety.

☐ **Other Regulatory Approvals:** Identify and obtain any other specific licenses or permits required for your business operations.

Chapter 11

Select Your Business Location

Key Takeaways

- Assessing Location Needs and Preferences

- Site Visits and Lease Negotiation

- Activity: Location Evaluation Checklist

Choosing the right location for your Party Planning Business is a critical step that can significantly influence your success. As a small business owner, you might be excited about the possibilities that lie ahead, but it's essential to approach this decision with careful consideration. A well-chosen location not only enhances your visibility but also makes it easier for potential clients to access your services.

Your business location should align with your target audience's preferences and behaviors. Are you aiming to attract clients from upscale neighborhoods, or do you want to cater to a more diverse demographic? Understanding your audience will help you identify the best areas to establish your presence. Additionally, consider the practical aspects such as accessibility, foot traffic, and proximity to suppliers and venues.

In this chapter, we will guide you through the process of assessing your location needs and preferences. You will learn how to conduct site visits, evaluate potential spaces, and negotiate leases effectively. This is your opportunity to create a welcoming environment that reflects your brand and resonates with your clients.

Remember, the right location can serve as a foundation for your business growth. It can enhance your brand image, attract more clients, and ultimately contribute to your bottom line. So, let's dive in and explore the key factors to consider when selecting the perfect location for your Party Planning Business!

Assessing Location Needs and Preferences

Choosing the right location for your Party Planning Business is crucial to its success. The location can influence your visibility, accessibility to clients, and overall operational efficiency. In this section, we will explore how to assess your location needs and preferences to ensure your business is set up for success.

1. **Identify Your Business Model**: Your business model will significantly impact your location needs. For instance, if you are primarily an online party planning service, you might not need a physical storefront. However, if you plan to host events or meet clients in person, a more accessible location will be essential. Consider whether you will need:

   - A dedicated office space for meetings and planning

   - A warehouse or storage area for inventory and supplies

   - A home office if you are starting small and want to minimize costs

2. **Analyze Your Target Market**: Understanding where your target audience is located is vital. If your services cater to families in a specific neighborhood, being close to that area can enhance your visibility and accessibility. Conduct market research to identify:

   - The demographics of your ideal clients

   - Where your competitors are located

   - Areas with high demand for party planning services

3. **Consider Accessibility**: Your location should be easy to access for both clients and suppliers. Consider the following factors:

   - **Transportation:** Is the location near public transport or major roads? This is especially important if you expect clients to visit your office or if you need to transport supplies.

   - **Parking:** Is there adequate parking available for clients and staff? A location with limited parking can deter potential clients.

4. **Evaluate Local Competition**: Understanding the competitive landscape can help you find a strategic location. Research how many similar businesses are in the area and what they offer. A location saturated with party planners might indicate high demand, but it could also mean stiff competition. Look for:

   - Areas with few competitors but high demand for party planning services

   - Unique locations that could set your business apart, such as near event venues or popular family attractions

5. **Assess the Cost of the Location**: Budget is a significant factor when selecting a location. Consider the following:

   - **Rent or Purchase Price:** Ensure that the cost aligns with your budget and projected revenue. Look for spaces that offer good value for money.

   - **Utilities and Maintenance:** Factor in additional costs such as utilities, maintenance, and property taxes when evaluating your budget.

6. **Future Growth Potential**: Finally, consider whether the location allows for future growth. As your business expands, you may need more space or to cater to a larger client base. Look for locations that can accommodate your business as it grows, such as:

- Spaces that can be easily modified or expanded

- Areas with increasing population or development plans that could enhance your client base

By thoroughly assessing your location needs and preferences, you can make an informed decision that supports the growth and success of your Party Planning Business. Take the time to explore various options and consider how each potential location aligns with your business goals.

Site Visits and Lease Negotiation

Choosing the right location for your Party Planning Business is crucial, as it can significantly impact your visibility, accessibility, and overall success. Once you have assessed your location needs and preferences, the next step is to conduct site visits and negotiate leases. This section will guide you through this process.

Site Visits

When visiting potential locations, consider the following factors:

- **Accessibility:** Ensure the location is easily accessible for both clients and suppliers. Look for proximity to major roads, public transport, and parking facilities.

- **Foot Traffic:** High foot traffic can be beneficial, especially if you plan to have a storefront or office accessible to walk-in clients. Consider visiting during peak hours to gauge the amount of foot traffic.

- **Space Layout:** Evaluate the layout of the space. Is it conducive to your business needs? Consider areas for meetings, storage, and any special requirements for your planning activities.

- **Surrounding Businesses:** Take note of nearby businesses. Are they complementary to your services? For example, being close to event venues, catering services, or florists can create synergies and referral opportunities.

During your site visits, take detailed notes and photographs to help you remember the specifics of each location. You may also want to create a checklist to ensure you assess all important aspects consistently.

Lease Negotiation

Once you have identified a location that meets your criteria, it's time to negotiate the lease. Here are some key points to consider:

- **Lease Terms:** Understand the length of the lease and the terms associated with it. A longer lease might provide stability, but it could also limit your flexibility. Consider starting with a shorter lease with options to extend.

- **Rent Costs:** Research the average rent prices in the area to ensure you are getting a fair deal. Don't hesitate to negotiate the rent, especially if you notice that the space has been vacant for a while.

- **Additional Costs:** Be aware of any additional costs that may come with the lease, such as maintenance fees, property taxes, or utilities. Ask the landlord to clarify what is included in the rent.

- **Improvements and Modifications:** If you need to make changes to the space to fit your business needs, discuss this with the landlord. Determine who will be responsible for the costs of renovations and whether you need permission for any modifications.

- **Exit Clause:** Ensure that the lease includes an exit clause that allows you to terminate the lease under specific conditions. This can provide you with flexibility if your business needs change.

It's advisable to consult with a real estate attorney or a commercial real estate agent during this process to ensure that you understand all legal implications and that your interests are protected.

In summary, conducting thorough site visits and negotiating favorable lease terms are essential steps in securing a location for your Party Planning Business. By being diligent and informed, you can set the foundation for a successful business operation.

Visit **www.BusinessBookstore.com/start** to download blank forms, etc.

Activity: Location Evaluation Checklist

Before finalizing your decision on a business location, it's crucial to thoroughly evaluate each potential site to ensure it aligns with your business needs and preferences. Use the following checklist during site visits to assess key factors and make an informed decision about the suitability of each location:

1. **Location and Accessibility:**

   ☐ Convenient proximity to target market

   ☐ Easy accessibility for customers and employees

   ☐ Visibility from main roads or thoroughfares

   ☐ Ample parking availability for customers and employees

2. **Physical Property Attributes:**

   ☐ Adequate space for current and future business needs

   ☐ Suitable layout and configuration for business operations

   ☐ Well-maintained condition of the property and facilities

   ☐ Compliance with zoning regulations and building codes

3. **Local Amenities and Infrastructure:**

☐ Availability of essential utilities (electricity, water, internet)

☐ Proximity to public transportation options, if applicable

☐ Access to amenities such as restaurants, banks, and other businesses

☐ Presence of supportive business infrastructure (business parks, incubators)

4. **Surrounding Environment and Community:**

☐ Compatibility with the overall aesthetic and vibe of the neighborhood

☐ Safety and security of the area, both during business hours and after-hours

☐ Presence of potential competitors and complementary businesses

☐ Engagement with the local community and potential for community support

5. **Lease Terms and Financial Considerations:**

☐ Affordability of rent and associated expenses (utilities, maintenance)

☐ Flexibility in lease terms (lease duration, renewal options)

☐ Transparency of lease agreements and any additional fees or charges

☐ Alignment with budgetary constraints and financial projection

6. **Landlord or Property Owner Relations:**

☐ Positive rapport and communication with the landlord or property owner

☐ Responsiveness to inquiries and concerns during the site visit

☐ Willingness to address potential issues and negotiate lease terms

7. **Overall Impression and Gut Feeling:**

☐ Personal gut feeling about the location's suitability for your business

☐ Overall impression of the property and its potential for success

☐ Alignment with your business's values, vision, and long-term goals

Once you have completed site visits and evaluated each potential location using this checklist, you will be better equipped to make an informed decision about the best location for your business.

Chapter 12

Manage Suppliers and Inventory

Key Takeaways

- Sourcing Suppliers and Negotiating Contracts

- Establishing Inventory Management Systems

- Activity: Supplier Evaluation Form

As you embark on your journey to establish a successful Party Planning Business, one of the critical components you'll need to master is managing suppliers and inventory. This chapter will guide you through the essential processes of sourcing quality suppliers and implementing effective inventory management systems. By doing so, you will ensure that your business runs smoothly and that you can consistently deliver exceptional services to your clients.

In the world of party planning, having reliable suppliers is paramount. They are the backbone of your business, providing everything from decorations and catering to venues and entertainment. Building strong relationships with your suppliers not only helps you secure the best prices but also ensures that you have access to high-quality products and services when you need them most.

Equally important is the management of your inventory. Efficient inventory management allows you to track what you have on hand, anticipate needs for upcoming events, and minimize waste. With the right systems in place, you can streamline your operations and focus on what you do best: creating memorable experiences for your clients.

In this chapter, we will explore:

- How to effectively source and negotiate with suppliers.

- Best practices for establishing inventory management systems.

- Tools and techniques to help you maintain control over your supplies.

Embrace the opportunity to refine these skills, as they will not only enhance your efficiency but also contribute significantly to your overall business success. Let's dive in and discover how to effectively manage your suppliers and inventory, setting the stage for a thriving party planning enterprise!

Sourcing Suppliers and Negotiating Contracts

When starting your Party Planning Business, sourcing suppliers and negotiating contracts are critical steps that can significantly impact your success. Suppliers provide the materials and services you need to execute your events, from decorations to catering. Establishing strong relationships with reliable suppliers can lead to better pricing, quality products, and improved service. Here's how to effectively source suppliers and negotiate contracts.

1. **Identify Your Needs**: Before you begin sourcing suppliers, clearly define what you need for your events. Consider the following:

   - *Types of Events:* Are you planning weddings, corporate events, birthday parties, or other types of gatherings? Each type may require different suppliers.

   - *Products and Services:* List out specific items or services you need, such as catering, floral arrangements, audiovisual equipment, or rental furniture.

   - *Budget:* Determine how much you can allocate for each category. This will help you filter potential suppliers based on your financial constraints.

2. **Research Potential Suppliers**: Once you have a clear understanding of your needs, start researching potential suppliers. Here are some strategies:

   - *Online Searches:* Use search engines and platforms like Yelp or Google Reviews to find suppliers in your area.

   - *Industry Contacts:* Reach out to fellow event planners or join industry groups. Networking can provide valuable recommendations.

   - *Trade Shows:* Attend local trade shows or expos related to event planning. These events are great for meeting suppliers and seeing their products firsthand.

3. **Evaluate Suppliers**: After compiling a list of potential suppliers, evaluate them based on several criteria:

    *   *Reputation:* Check online reviews and ask for references. A supplier's reputation can indicate their reliability and quality of service.

    *   *Experience:* Consider how long the supplier has been in business and their experience with events similar to yours.

    *   *Pricing:* Request quotes from multiple suppliers to compare pricing. Be cautious of prices that seem too low, as they may reflect lower quality.

4. **Negotiate Contracts**: Once you've selected your preferred suppliers, it's time to negotiate contracts. Here are some tips:

    *   *Be Transparent:* Clearly communicate your needs and expectations. This will help avoid misunderstandings later on.

    *   *Discuss Terms:* Pay attention to key contract elements, including pricing, payment terms, cancellation policies, and delivery timelines.

    *   *Ask for Discounts:* Don't hesitate to ask for discounts, especially if you're ordering in bulk or planning multiple events with the same supplier.

    *   *Review the Fine Print:* Always read the contract carefully. Ensure that all verbal agreements are documented in writing.

5. **Build Long-Term Relationships**: After securing your suppliers, work on building long-term relationships. Regular communication and feedback can strengthen these partnerships, leading to better service and pricing in the future. Consider the following:

   - *Regular Check-Ins:* Touch base with suppliers periodically to maintain the relationship.

   - *Feedback:* Provide constructive feedback to help suppliers improve their services.

   - *Referral Opportunities:* If you're satisfied with their service, refer them to other planners or clients, which can foster goodwill.

By carefully sourcing suppliers and negotiating contracts, you can create a solid foundation for your Party Planning Business, ensuring that your events run smoothly and successfully.

Establishing Inventory Management Systems

Establishing an effective inventory management system is crucial for the success of your Party Planning Business. An organized inventory system helps ensure that you have the necessary supplies on hand for each event, minimizes waste, and optimizes your budget. Here are key steps and considerations for setting up your inventory management system:

1. **Identify Your Inventory Needs**: Begin by making a comprehensive list of all the items you will need for your Party Planning Business. This may include:

   - Decorations (balloons, banners, centerpieces)

   - Tableware (plates, cups, utensils)

   - Furniture (tables, chairs, linens)

   - Audio/Visual equipment (speakers, microphones, projectors)

   - Party supplies (favors, games, activities)

By clearly identifying what you need, you can streamline your purchasing process and ensure you have everything required for your events.

2. **Choose an Inventory Management Method**: There are several methods to manage your inventory, and the right choice will depend on the size of your business and your personal preferences. Here are a few options:

   - **Manual Tracking:** This method involves using spreadsheets to track inventory levels, orders, and sales. While it can be effective for small businesses, it may become cumbersome as your inventory grows.

   - **Inventory Management Software:** Consider investing in software specifically designed for inventory management. These tools can automate tracking, provide real-time updates, and generate reports. Popular options include *Square for Retail*, *Zoho Inventory*, and *QuickBooks Commerce*.

   - **Barcode Systems:** Using barcodes can significantly speed up the inventory process. By scanning items as they are added or removed from inventory, you can maintain accurate records with less effort.

3. **Set Par Levels**: Par levels are the minimum quantity of each item that you should have on hand. Setting these levels helps you avoid stockouts and ensures you can meet client demands. For example, if you typically need 50 tablecloths for an event, setting a par level of 60 ensures you have enough to cover unexpected needs or last-minute bookings.

4. **Conduct Regular Inventory Audits**: Regular audits are essential to ensure that your inventory records match the actual stock on hand. Schedule periodic checks—monthly or quarterly—to count items and reconcile any discrepancies. This practice can help catch issues early, such as theft, damage, or miscounting.

5. **Track Inventory Usage**: Keep records of how much inventory you use for each event. This data will help you analyze trends and make informed purchasing decisions. For example, if you notice that certain decorations are consistently popular, you may want to stock up on those items.

6. **Build Relationships with Suppliers**: Establishing strong relationships with your suppliers can lead to better prices, priority service, and flexibility in ordering. Communicate your needs clearly, and don't hesitate to negotiate terms that work for both parties. Consider creating a preferred vendor list to streamline your procurement process.

By implementing these strategies for establishing an inventory management system, you can enhance your efficiency, reduce costs, and ensure that your Party Planning Business runs smoothly. A well-organized inventory will allow you to focus on what truly matters: creating unforgettable experiences for your clients.

Visit **www.BusinessBookstore.com/start** for a list of suppliers.

Activity: Supplier Evaluation Form

Instructions:

Before selecting suppliers for your business, it's essential to thoroughly evaluate their capabilities, reliability, and compatibility with your business needs. Use the following Supplier Evaluation Form to assess potential suppliers based on key criteria discussed in previous chapters. Rate each criterion on a scale of 1 to 5, with 1 being the lowest and 5 being the highest, and provide comments or additional notes as needed. This evaluation will help you make informed decisions and choose suppliers that align with your business goals and requirements.

Supplier Evaluation Form

1. Supplier Information:

- Name of Supplier: _____

- Contact Person: _____

- Contact Information: _____

- Industry Experience: [Rating: 1-5] _____

   Comments: _____

- Reputation and References: [Rating: 1-5] _____

   Comments: _____

- Financial Stability: [Rating: 1-5] _____

   Comments: _____

2. Product Quality and Consistency:

- Quality Control Measures: [Rating: 1-5] _____

  Comments: _____

- Compliance with Standards: [Rating: 1-5] _____

  Comments: _____

- Product Warranty/Guarantee: [Rating: 1-5] _____

  Comments: _____

3. Price and Terms:

- Pricing Competitiveness: [Rating: 1-5] _____

  Comments: _____

- Payment Terms and Conditions: [Rating: 1-5] _____

  Comments: _____

- Volume Discounts: [Rating: 1-5] _____

  Comments: _____

4. Delivery and Lead Times:

- On-Time Delivery Performance: [Rating: 1-5] _____

  Comments: _____

- Lead Time for Orders: [Rating: 1-5] _____

  Comments: _____

- Shipping and Handling: [Rating: 1-5] _____

    Comments: _____

5. Customer Service and Support:

  - Responsiveness to Inquiries: [Rating: 1-5] _____

    Comments: _____

  - Problem Resolution: [Rating: 1-5] _____

    Comments: _____

  - Availability of Support: [Rating: 1-5] _____

    Comments: _____

6. Overall Satisfaction:

  - Overall Satisfaction with Supplier: [Rating: 1-5] _____

    Comments: _____

Conclusion:

After completing the Supplier Evaluation Form for each potential supplier, review the ratings and comments to identify strengths, weaknesses, and areas for improvement. Use this information to make informed decisions about selecting suppliers that best meet your business requirements and objectives. Remember to revisit and update the evaluation periodically to ensure ongoing supplier performance and satisfaction.

Chapter 13

Protect Your Business With Insurance

Key Takeaways

- Understanding Business Insurance Needs

- Choosing the Right Insurance Policies

- Activity: Business Insurance Checklist

As a small business owner, you have embarked on an exciting journey filled with opportunities and challenges. One of the most critical aspects of running your own Party Planning Business is ensuring that you are adequately protected against unforeseen risks. While you focus on creating memorable events for your clients, it is essential to safeguard your business from potential liabilities that could threaten its success.

Insurance is not just an expense; it is a vital investment in your business's future. By understanding the different types of insurance available and selecting the right policies, you can protect your assets, manage risks, and gain peace of mind. This chapter will guide you through the various insurance options tailored for your Party Planning Business, helping you make informed decisions that align with your unique needs.

In this chapter, we will cover:

- **Understanding Business Insurance Needs:** Learn about the specific risks associated with the party planning industry and how insurance can mitigate those risks.

- **Choosing the Right Insurance Policies:** Explore the different types of insurance, including general liability, professional liability, and property insurance, to determine what's best for your business.

By taking the time to protect your business with the right insurance, you are not only safeguarding your investment but also building a solid foundation for future growth. Let's dive into the world of business insurance and ensure that your party planning venture is secure and thriving!

Understanding Business Insurance Needs

Starting your own Party Planning Business can be an exciting venture, but it also comes with its fair share of risks. Understanding your business insurance needs is crucial to protect your investment, your clients, and yourself. This section will explore the various types of insurance that are essential for party planners and how they can safeguard your business.

First and foremost, it's important to recognize that different businesses have different insurance requirements based on their specific activities and risks. As a party planner, you will be responsible for organizing events, which can involve a range of services from venue selection to catering and entertainment. Each of these services may expose you to potential liabilities, making it essential to have the right coverage.

Here are some key types of insurance you should consider:

- **General Liability Insurance:** This is one of the most important types of insurance for any business. It protects you against claims of bodily injury, property damage, and personal injury that may occur during an event. For example, if a guest trips over a decoration you set up and gets injured, general liability insurance can help cover medical expenses and legal fees.

- **Professional Liability Insurance:** Also known as errors and omissions insurance, this coverage protects you against claims of negligence or mistakes in the services you provide. If a client claims that your planning led to a significant issue at their event, this insurance can help defend you in court and cover any settlements.

- **Commercial Property Insurance:** If you have a physical location for your business or store equipment, this insurance protects your property against theft, fire, or other damages. For instance, if your office is damaged in a storm, commercial property insurance can help you recover the costs of repairs or replacements.

- **Workers' Compensation Insurance:** If you hire employees, this insurance is often required by law. It covers medical expenses and lost wages for employees who are injured on the job. For example, if a staff member gets injured while setting up an event, workers' compensation insurance ensures they receive the necessary care and compensation.

- **Event Cancellation Insurance:** This type of insurance can be particularly valuable for party planners. It protects against financial losses due to unforeseen cancellations, such as extreme weather or other emergencies. For example, if a wedding is canceled due to a natural disaster, this insurance can help recover non-refundable expenses.

When assessing your insurance needs, consider the following steps:

- **Evaluate Risks:** Conduct a thorough assessment of the potential risks associated with your business activities. Consider factors such as the types of events you plan, the venues you work with, and any subcontractors you may hire.

- **Consult with an Insurance Agent:** Speak with a licensed insurance agent who specializes in business insurance. They can help you understand the specific coverage options available and tailor a policy that meets your needs.

- **Review and Update Regularly:** As your business grows and evolves, your insurance needs may change. Regularly review your policies to ensure you have adequate coverage as you expand your services or take on new clients.

In conclusion, understanding your business insurance needs is a vital step in establishing a successful Party Planning Business. By investing in the right insurance coverage, you can protect yourself from potential liabilities and focus on what you do best—creating memorable events for your clients.

Choosing the Right Insurance Policies

Choosing the right insurance policies for your Party Planning Business is crucial for protecting your investment and ensuring your operations run smoothly. Insurance not only provides financial security against unexpected events but also enhances your business's credibility with clients. Here are some essential types of insurance to consider:

- **General Liability Insurance:** This is one of the most important types of insurance for any business, including party planning. It covers claims related to bodily injury, property damage, and personal injury that may occur during your events. For instance, if a guest trips over a decoration and gets injured, general liability insurance can help cover medical expenses and legal fees.

- **Professional Liability Insurance:** Also known as errors and omissions insurance, this policy protects you against claims of negligence, mistakes, or failure to deliver services as promised. If a client claims that you did not meet their expectations or that your planning led to a significant issue during their event, this insurance will help cover legal costs and potential settlements.

- **Property Insurance:** If you own or lease office space and have equipment, supplies, or inventory, property insurance is essential. It protects your physical assets from risks such as theft, fire, or natural disasters. For example, if your office is damaged in a storm, property insurance can help you recover the costs of repairs and replacement of damaged items.

- **Workers' Compensation Insurance:** If you hire employees or contractors, workers' compensation insurance is often required by law. This insurance covers medical expenses and lost wages for employees who are injured on the job. For instance, if a staff member is injured while setting up an event, this insurance will ensure they receive the necessary medical care without financial burden.

- **Event Cancellation Insurance:** This type of insurance is particularly relevant for party planners, as it covers financial losses if an event is canceled due to unforeseen circumstances, such as extreme weather or a venue suddenly becoming unavailable. For example, if a wedding is canceled due to a natural disaster, this insurance can help recover deposits and other expenses incurred.

- **Commercial Auto Insurance:** If you use a vehicle for business purposes, such as transporting supplies or staff to events, commercial auto insurance is necessary. This policy covers accidents and damages related to your business vehicle, ensuring that you are protected while on the road.

When selecting insurance policies, here are some steps to follow:

- **Assess Your Needs:** Evaluate the specific risks associated with your business. Consider the types of events you plan, the number of employees you have, and whether you own or lease property.

- **Shop Around:** Obtain quotes from multiple insurance providers. Compare coverage options, premiums, and customer service ratings to find the best fit for your business.

- **Consult an Insurance Agent:** An experienced insurance agent can help you navigate the complexities of business insurance. They can recommend policies tailored to your specific needs and ensure you have adequate coverage.

- **Review Policies Regularly:** As your business grows and changes, your insurance needs may evolve. Regularly review your policies to ensure you have the right coverage in place.

In conclusion, investing in the right insurance policies is a vital step in safeguarding your Party Planning Business. By understanding your risks and choosing appropriate coverage, you can focus on creating memorable events while ensuring your business is protected from unforeseen challenges.

Visit **www.BusinessBookstore.com/start** for a list of insurance agencies.

Activity: Business Insurance Checklist

Assess Your Insurance Needs

Identify Potential Risks

- ☐ List the types of risks your business may face (e.g., property damage, liability, employee injuries).
- ☐ Consider industry-specific risks.

Evaluate Coverage Requirements

- ☐ Determine which types of insurance are legally required in your location (e.g., workers' compensation).
- ☐ Identify additional coverage that might be beneficial (e.g., cyber liability insurance).

Research Insurance Providers

Compare Multiple Providers

- ☐ List at least three insurance providers you will consider.
- ☐ Check each provider's reputation and customer reviews.

Request Quotes

- ☐ Obtain detailed quotes from each provider for the types of coverage you need.
- ☐ Ensure quotes include coverage limits, deductibles, and premiums.

Evaluate Insurance Policies

Coverage Options

☐ Compare the types of coverage offered by each provider.

☐ Ensure policies cover all identified risks and requirements.

Policy Terms and Conditions

☐ Review exclusions and limitations in each policy.

☐ Check for any additional fees or clauses that could impact coverage.

Make a Decision

Cost vs. Coverage

☐ Balance the cost of premiums against the level of coverage provided.

☐ Consider any potential discounts for bundling policies.

Provider Reliability

☐ Evaluate the reliability and financial stability of each provider.

☐ Consider the provider's customer service and claims handling process.

Purchase and Review

Select Your Policies

☐ Choose the insurance policies that best meet your business needs.

☐ Ensure you understand the coverage details and terms.

Regularly Review Coverage

☐ Set reminders to review your insurance coverage annually.

☐ Adjust policies as your business grows or changes.

Chapter 14

Hire and Train Your Team

Key Takeaways

- Identifying Hiring Needs and Job Roles

- Recruiting and Interviewing Candidates

- Activity: Hiring Process Checklist

As you embark on the journey of building your Party Planning Business, one of the most crucial steps is to hire and train a team that shares your vision and values. Your team will be the backbone of your operations, playing a vital role in delivering exceptional experiences to your clients. The right people not only enhance your service offerings but also contribute to a positive work environment that fosters creativity and collaboration.

Hiring is not just about filling positions; it's about finding individuals who align with your business goals and culture. By carefully selecting team members who are passionate about event planning and customer service, you can create a cohesive unit that works seamlessly together. Remember, a strong team can elevate your business to new heights, allowing you to take on larger projects and grow your reputation in the industry.

Training is equally important. Providing your team with the necessary skills and knowledge will empower them to perform their roles effectively and confidently. This investment in their development not only enhances their performance but also boosts morale and job satisfaction. A well-trained team is more likely to provide outstanding service, leading to repeat business and referrals.

In this chapter, we will explore the essential steps to identify your hiring needs, recruit the right candidates, and develop a training program that equips your team for success. By focusing on these key areas, you are setting the foundation for a thriving business that can adapt and grow in the ever-changing landscape of party planning.

Let's dive in and build a team that will help your vision come to life!

Identifying Hiring Needs and Job Roles

As you embark on your journey to establish a successful Party Planning Business, one of the crucial steps is identifying your hiring needs and defining job roles within your organization. The right team can significantly impact the quality of your services, customer satisfaction, and overall business growth. This section will guide you through the process of determining what roles you need to fill and how to articulate those roles effectively.

Start by assessing the core functions of your business. In party planning, these may include:

- **Event Coordination:** This role involves managing the logistics of events, from planning timelines to coordinating with vendors and ensuring everything runs smoothly on the day of the event.

- **Marketing and Sales:** A dedicated marketing professional can help promote your services, manage social media accounts, and develop marketing strategies to attract new clients.

- **Customer Service:** Excellent customer service is vital in the event planning industry. A customer service representative can handle inquiries, follow-ups, and ensure client satisfaction throughout the planning process.

- **Design and Décor Specialist:** If your business focuses on event styling, hiring a designer who understands aesthetics, themes, and current trends can enhance the overall experience for your clients.

- **Finance and Administration:** Managing budgets, invoicing, and financial planning is essential for keeping your business financially healthy. Consider hiring someone with financial expertise to oversee these aspects.

Once you have outlined the necessary functions, it's time to define specific job roles. Consider the following steps:

1. **Job Descriptions:** Create detailed job descriptions for each role. Include responsibilities, required skills, and qualifications. For example, a job description for an Event Coordinator might include tasks such as:

    *   Planning event timelines and schedules.

    *   Coordinating with vendors and suppliers.

    *   Managing budgets and ensuring cost-effective solutions.

    *   Overseeing event setup and breakdown.

2. **Identify Required Skills:** Determine the skills necessary for each position. For instance, an Event Coordinator should possess strong organizational skills, attention to detail, and the ability to multitask effectively.

3. **Assess Workload:** Evaluate the volume of work your business is likely to generate. This will help you decide whether to hire full-time employees, part-time staff, or freelancers. For example, during peak seasons, you may need additional event coordinators or assistants to manage increased demand.

4. **Consider Cultural Fit:** Beyond skills and experience, it's essential to find individuals who align with your company's values and culture. This can enhance teamwork and improve overall morale.

As you begin the hiring process, think about how you will attract the right candidates. Utilize platforms like job boards, social media, and networking events to reach potential employees. Additionally, consider offering internships or apprenticeships to those looking to gain experience in the event planning industry.

In summary, identifying hiring needs and defining job roles is a critical step in building a successful Party Planning Business. By clearly outlining the functions your business requires and articulating specific roles, you will be better equipped to find the right team members who can help bring your vision to life.

Recruiting and Interviewing Candidates

Recruiting and interviewing candidates is a critical step in building a successful Party Planning Business. The right team can help you execute events flawlessly, maintain client relationships, and uphold your brand's reputation. Here's a structured approach to ensure you attract and select the best candidates for your business.

1. **Define Your Hiring Needs**: Before you start the recruiting process, it's essential to clearly define the roles you need to fill. Consider the following:

   - **Job Roles:** Identify specific positions such as event planners, coordinators, assistants, or marketing specialists. Outline their responsibilities and how they contribute to the overall success of your business.

   - **Skills and Qualifications:** Determine the skills necessary for each role. For instance, an event planner may need strong organizational skills, creativity, and experience in vendor management.

   - **Experience Level:** Decide whether you want to hire experienced professionals or if entry-level candidates with potential are acceptable.

2. **Create a Compelling Job Description**: A well-crafted job description not only outlines the role but also attracts suitable candidates. Include the following elements:

   - **Job Title:** Use a clear and specific title.

   - **Responsibilities:** List key tasks and expectations.

   - **Qualifications:** Specify required skills, experience, and educational background.

   - **Company Culture:** Provide insight into your business values and work environment to attract candidates who align with your ethos.

3. **Utilize Multiple Recruitment Channels**: To reach a diverse pool of candidates, consider using various recruitment channels:

    *   **Online Job Boards:** Websites like Indeed, Glassdoor, and LinkedIn can help you post your job openings and reach a broad audience.

    *   **Social Media:** Leverage platforms like Facebook, Instagram, and Twitter/X to share job postings and engage with potential candidates.

    *   **Networking Events:** Attend industry-related events to meet potential candidates in person and build relationships.

    *   **Referrals:** Encourage current employees or industry contacts to refer candidates. Offering a referral bonus can motivate them to help you find the right fit.

4. **Conducting Interviews**: Once you've shortlisted candidates, it's time to conduct interviews. Here are some tips to ensure a successful interview process:

    *   **Prepare Questions:** Develop a list of questions that assess both technical skills and cultural fit. For example, ask about their experience managing events, handling last-minute changes, or working with vendors.

    *   **Behavioral Questions:** Use behavioral interview techniques to understand how candidates have handled situations in the past. Questions like "Can you describe a time when an event didn't go as planned? How did you handle it?" can provide valuable insights.

    *   **Assess Soft Skills:** In the party planning industry, soft skills such as communication, problem-solving, and teamwork are crucial. Pay attention to how candidates interact with you during the interview.

5. **Follow Up and Make Your Decision**: After the interviews, take the time to evaluate each candidate. Consider their skills, experience, and how well they align with your company culture. Once you've made your decision, promptly follow up with all candidates, thanking them for their time and informing them of your choice.

By effectively recruiting and interviewing candidates, you can build a strong team that will help your Party Planning Business thrive. Remember, investing time in this process will pay off in the long run, as the right hires contribute significantly to your business's success.

Visit **www.BusinessBookstore.com/start** to download blank staffing forms.

Activity: Hiring Process Checklist

Congratulations on taking the next step in building your dream team! Use this checklist to guide you through the hiring process and ensure you find the best candidates for your small business.

1. **Define Hiring Needs:**

    ☐ Identify the roles and positions you need to fill.

    ☐ Determine the qualifications, skills, and experience required for each role.

    ☐ Set clear objectives and expectations for the new hires.

2. **Craft Job Descriptions:**

    ☐ Write clear and concise job descriptions for each role.

    ☐ Highlight the responsibilities, qualifications, and key competencies required.

    ☐ Include information about your company culture, values, and mission to attract the right candidates.

3. **Choose Recruitment Channels:**

    ☐ Select appropriate recruitment channels such as job boards, social media, and professional networks.

    ☐ Utilize employee referrals and networking to reach potential candidates.

    ☐ Consider using recruitment agencies or outsourcing if needed.

4. **Screen Resumes and Applications:**

☐ Review resumes, cover letters, and applications to shortlist qualified candidates.

☐ Look for relevant skills, experience, and alignment with your company culture.

☐ Keep track of candidates' information and communication for future reference.

5. **Conduct Interviews:**

☐ Schedule interviews with shortlisted candidates.

☐ Prepare a list of structured interview questions tailored to each role.

☐ Conduct interviews to assess candidates' qualifications, experience, and cultural fit.

6. **Assess Candidates:**

☐ Evaluate candidates based on their skills, experience, and alignment with your company values.

☐ Consider conducting additional assessments or tests if necessary.

☐ Gather feedback from other team members involved in the interview process.

7. **Extend Job Offers:**

☐ Select the top candidate for each role.

☐ Prepare and extend job offers to selected candidates.

☐ Negotiate terms of employment, including salary, benefits, and start date.

8. **Onboarding Process:**

☐ Develop an onboarding plan to welcome new hires and integrate them into your team.

☐ Provide necessary training, resources, and support to help new hires succeed.

☐ Communicate expectations and goals for the new hires' roles.

9. **Follow-Up and Feedback:**

☐ Follow up with candidates who were not selected and provide constructive feedback if possible.

☐ Monitor the performance and progress of new hires during their probationary period.

☐ Seek feedback from new hires to continuously improve your hiring process.

10. **Continuous Improvement:**

☐ Reflect on the hiring process and identify areas for improvement.

☐ Solicit feedback from your team and candidates to enhance the recruitment experience.

☐ Update job descriptions, interview questions, and recruitment strategies based on lessons learned.

Remember to customize this checklist to fit your specific hiring needs and adapt it as your small business grows and evolves. Good luck with your hiring process!

Chapter 15

Set Up Your Technology

Key Takeaways

- Assessing Technology Requirements

- Selecting Software and Tools

- Activity: Technology Needs Assessment

Welcome to Chapter 15: **Set Up Your Technology**. In today's fast-paced digital world, having the right technology in place is essential for the success of your Party Planning Business. The tools you choose can streamline your operations, enhance your communication, and elevate the overall experience for your clients. As a small business owner, embracing technology may seem daunting, but it is also an exciting opportunity to innovate and improve your processes.

In this chapter, we will explore the various technology requirements your business may need, from project management software to customer relationship management (CRM) systems. Understanding these tools will empower you to make informed decisions that align with your business goals. Remember, you don't need to implement everything at once; start small and scale your technology stack as your business grows.

Additionally, we will discuss how to select the right software and tools that fit your unique needs. Whether you are managing client bookings, coordinating events, or tracking expenses, the right technology can help you work more efficiently and effectively.

As you embark on this journey, keep in mind that technology is not just about the tools themselves but how you leverage them to create value for your clients and streamline your operations. Embrace this chapter as a stepping stone toward building a robust technological foundation for your Party Planning Business. Let's dive in and explore how you can set up your technology to thrive in this competitive industry!

Assessing Technology Requirements

As you embark on your journey to start a Party Planning Business, assessing your technology requirements is crucial for streamlining operations, enhancing communication, and improving overall efficiency. In today's digital age, the right technology can help you manage your business more effectively, allowing you to focus on creativity and client satisfaction.

To begin assessing your technology needs, consider the following key areas:

- **Business Management Software:** This can include project management tools, scheduling software, and customer relationship management (CRM) systems. For instance, tools like *Trello* or *Asana* can help you manage tasks and timelines for different events, while *HubSpot* or *Zoho CRM* can assist in managing client interactions and tracking leads.

- **Communication Tools:** Effective communication is vital in party planning, as you will need to coordinate with clients, vendors, and your team. Consider using platforms like *Slack* for team communication and *Zoom* or *Google Meet* for virtual meetings with clients or vendors. These tools facilitate quick and efficient discussions, ensuring everyone is on the same page.

- **Financial Management Software:** Keeping track of your finances is essential for any business. Software like *QuickBooks* or *Xero* can help you manage invoices, expenses, and financial reporting. This will help you maintain a clear picture of your cash flow and profitability, which is vital for long-term success.

- **Event Planning Software:** Specialized software can streamline the event planning process. Consider using platforms like *Eventbrite* for ticketing and registration, or *Social Tables* for managing seating arrangements and floor plans. These tools can save you time and reduce the likelihood of errors during the planning process.

- **Website and Online Presence:** A professional website is essential for attracting clients. Ensure your website is user-friendly, mobile-responsive, and includes essential information about your services, portfolio, and contact details. You may also want to consider a booking system integrated into your website, which allows clients to schedule consultations or events directly.

- **Social Media Management Tools:** Social media is a powerful marketing tool for party planners. Tools like *Hootsuite* or *Buffer* can help you schedule posts across different platforms, track engagement, and analyze performance. This will enable you to maintain an active online presence without overwhelming your schedule.

Once you have identified the areas where technology can support your business, it's time to evaluate specific tools and platforms. Here are some steps to guide you:

- **Research Options:** Look for software solutions that cater specifically to the party planning industry or those that are widely used by small businesses. Read reviews, compare features, and consider trial versions to see what works best for you.

- **Budget Considerations:** Assess the costs associated with each technology solution. Determine what fits within your budget while still meeting your needs. Keep in mind that investing in quality tools can save you time and money in the long run.

- **Scalability:** As your business grows, your technology needs may change. Choose solutions that can scale with your business, allowing you to add features or users as needed.

By carefully assessing your technology requirements and selecting the right tools, you can set a strong foundation for your Party Planning Business. The right technology will not only enhance your efficiency but also improve your client interactions, ultimately contributing to your success.

Selecting Software and Tools

In today's digital age, selecting the right software and tools is crucial for the success of your Party Planning Business. The right technology can streamline your processes, enhance communication, and improve your overall efficiency. Here are key categories of software and tools to consider when setting up your business:

1. **Project Management Tools**: Project management software helps you organize tasks, deadlines, and team collaboration. This is particularly important in party planning, where multiple elements need to come together seamlessly. Some popular options include:

    *   *Trello*: A user-friendly platform that uses boards and cards to manage tasks visually.

    *   *Asana*: Offers more robust project tracking features, allowing you to assign tasks and set deadlines.

    *   *Monday.com*: A highly customizable tool that can adapt to various workflows, making it suitable for different types of events.

2. **Communication Tools**: Effective communication is vital for coordinating with clients, vendors, and team members. Consider these tools:

    *   *Slack*: A messaging platform that allows for organized conversations through channels, making it easy to keep discussions focused.

    *   *Zoom*: Ideal for virtual meetings and consultations, especially if your clients are not local.

    *   *Email Marketing Software*: Tools like Mailchimp or Constant Contact can help you maintain communication with clients and send updates or newsletters.

3. **Event Management Software**: Specific event management tools can help you streamline the planning process from start to finish. These platforms often include features for ticketing, RSVPs, and guest management:

    *   *Eventbrite*: Great for ticketing and managing registrations for events.

    *   *Whova*: Offers comprehensive event management features, including attendee engagement tools.

    *   *Social Tables*: Excellent for managing seating arrangements and floor plans for events.

4. **Financial Management Tools**: Managing your finances is essential for the sustainability of your business. Consider using:

    *   *QuickBooks*: A widely used accounting software that helps you track expenses, send invoices, and manage payroll.

    *   *FreshBooks*: Designed for small businesses, it offers easy invoicing and expense tracking.

5. **Design and Presentation Tools**: Visual presentation is key in party planning, whether you're creating proposals or marketing materials. Tools to consider include:

    *   *Canva*: A user-friendly graphic design tool that allows you to create stunning visuals without needing advanced design skills.

    *   *Adobe Spark*: Perfect for creating web pages, videos, and graphics that showcase your events.

6. **Social Media Management Tools**: Promoting your business on social media is essential. Use tools like:

- *Hootsuite*: Manage multiple social media accounts from one dashboard and schedule posts in advance.

- *Buffer*: Another excellent option for scheduling and analyzing social media performance.

When selecting software and tools, consider your specific needs, budget, and the scale of your operations. Many of these platforms offer free trials, allowing you to test them before making a commitment. By investing in the right technology, you'll set your Party Planning Business up for success, ensuring that you can focus on what you do best: creating unforgettable events.

> Visit **www.BusinessBookstore.com/start** for a list of software providers.

Activity: Technology Needs Assessment

Before selecting software and tools for your small business, it's essential to assess your technology needs and requirements. Use the following checklist to evaluate your current technology infrastructure and identify areas where new software solutions could improve efficiency and support your business goals.

1. **Current Technology Infrastructure:**

   - ☐ Assess the current technology tools and systems used in your business, including hardware, software, and networking equipment.
   - ☐ Identify any gaps or limitations in your existing technology infrastructure that may be hindering productivity or growth.

2. **Business Goals and Objectives:**

   - ☐ Define your business goals and objectives, including short-term and long-term targets for growth, revenue, and customer satisfaction.
   - ☐ Determine how technology can support your business goals and enhance your ability to achieve success.

3. **Operational Needs and Challenges:**

   - ☐ Identify specific operational needs and challenges within your business, such as inventory management, customer relationship management, or financial reporting.
   - ☐ Consider how technology solutions can address these operational needs and challenges to streamline workflows and improve efficiency.

4. **Employee Requirements:**

- ☐ Evaluate the technology requirements of your employees, including software tools and systems needed to perform their roles effectively.
- ☐ Consider factors such as remote work capabilities, collaboration tools, and training needs to support your workforce.

5. **Customer Experience:**

- ☐ Assess the current customer experience provided by your business, including interactions through various channels such as your website, social media, and customer service.
- ☐ Identify opportunities to enhance the customer experience through technology solutions such as e-commerce platforms, customer relationship management (CRM) software, or communication tools.

6. **Security and Data Protection:**

- ☐ Review your current security measures and protocols to protect sensitive business data and customer information.
- ☐ Identify any potential vulnerabilities or areas of concern that need to be addressed with technology solutions such as cybersecurity software or data encryption tools.

7. **Budget and Resources:**

- ☐ Determine your budget and resources available for investing in new technology solutions.
- ☐ Consider factors such as upfront costs, ongoing maintenance fees, and potential return on investment (ROI) when evaluating technology options.

8. **Integration and Scalability:**

   ☐ Assess the compatibility and integration capabilities of potential technology solutions with your existing systems and tools.

   ☐ Consider the scalability of the software and tools to accommodate future growth and expansion of your business.

9. **Vendor Selection Criteria:**

   ☐ Define criteria for selecting technology vendors, including factors such as reputation, reliability, customer support, and user satisfaction.

   ☐ Research potential vendors and evaluate them against your selection criteria to identify the best fit for your business.

10. **Final Assessment and Prioritization:**

    ☐ Review your technology needs assessment and prioritize areas where new technology solutions are most needed and will have the greatest impact on your business.

    ☐ Develop a plan for implementing new technology solutions based on your assessment and prioritize them according to your business goals and objectives.

Conclusion:

Completing this technology needs assessment will provide valuable insights into your business's technology requirements and help you make informed decisions when selecting software and tools to support your operations. Use the information gathered from this assessment to guide your technology strategy and investment decisions for optimal business performance and growth.

Chapter 16

Prepare Your Launch Plan

Key Takeaways

- Setting Launch Goals and Objectives

- Creating Launch Timeline and Marketing Strategy

- Activity: Business Launch Checklist

Congratulations on reaching this pivotal chapter in your journey to launch your own Party Planning Business! As you prepare to introduce your services to the world, it's essential to have a well-structured launch plan. This plan will serve as your roadmap, guiding you through the final steps before opening your doors to clients. A successful launch can set the tone for your business, attracting customers and establishing your brand in the competitive marketplace.

In this chapter, we will explore the key components of an effective launch plan. You will learn how to:

- **Set clear launch goals and objectives:** Defining what success looks like for your launch will help you stay focused and motivated.

- **Create a detailed launch timeline:** Organizing tasks and deadlines ensures that you are well-prepared and can execute your plan seamlessly.

- **Develop a marketing strategy:** Promoting your business effectively will help you reach your target audience and generate excitement around your launch.

Remember, the effort you put into planning your launch will pay off in the long run. A well-executed launch not only creates buzz but also fosters trust and credibility with your potential clients. As you move forward, embrace the excitement and challenges that come with this phase. You are not just starting a business; you are building a dream. Let's dive into the essential steps to prepare your launch plan and ensure your Party Planning Business gets off to a fantastic start!

Setting Launch Goals and Objectives

Setting launch goals and objectives is a crucial step in ensuring the success of your Party Planning Business. These goals provide a clear direction and help you measure progress as you prepare for your launch. Well-defined objectives can also motivate your team and keep you focused on your priorities. Here's how to effectively set your goals and objectives.

1. **Understand the Difference Between Goals and Objectives**: While the terms "goals" and "objectives" are often used interchangeably, they have distinct meanings:

   - **Goals** are broad, overarching targets you aim to achieve. They are typically long-term and can be somewhat abstract. For example, "Establish a reputable Party Planning Business within the first year."

   - **Objectives** are specific, measurable actions that support your goals. They are usually short-term and clearly defined. For example, "Book 10 events in the first three months of operation."

2. **Use the SMART Criteria**: To ensure your goals and objectives are effective, use the SMART criteria:

   - **Specific:** Clearly define what you want to achieve. Instead of saying "increase customers," say "gain 20 new clients by the end of the first quarter."

   - **Measurable:** Include metrics to track progress. For instance, "Increase social media followers by 50% within six months."

   - **Achievable:** Set realistic goals that are attainable. If you're just starting, aim for a number of events that won't overwhelm you.

   - **Relevant:** Ensure your objectives align with your overall business vision. For example, "Launch a referral program to encourage word-of-mouth marketing."

- **Time-bound:** Set a deadline for achieving your goals. For example, "Complete the website launch by the end of the first month."

3. **Break Down Goals into Actionable Steps**: Once you have set your goals and objectives, break them down into smaller, actionable tasks. This makes them less daunting and easier to manage. For instance:

   - For the goal of booking 10 events, your actionable steps could include:

   - Networking with local vendors and venues.

   - Creating promotional materials to distribute.

   - Setting up a launch event to showcase your services.

   - For increasing social media followers, actionable steps might include:

   - Creating a content calendar for consistent posting.

   - Engaging with followers regularly through comments and messages.

   - Running a targeted ad campaign to reach potential clients.

4. **Review and Adjust Regularly**: As you work towards your launch, regularly review your goals and objectives. Assess what is working and what may need adjustment. This flexibility allows you to respond to challenges or opportunities that arise. For example, if you find that social media engagement is lower than expected, you might need to revise your content strategy or explore new platforms.

By setting clear launch goals and objectives, you create a structured path toward the successful launch of your Party Planning Business. This strategic approach not only helps you stay organized but also enhances your chances of achieving your desired outcomes. Remember, the key to success lies in planning, execution, and the ability to adapt as needed.

Creating Launch Timeline and Marketing Strategy

Launching your Party Planning Business successfully requires a well-structured timeline and a comprehensive marketing strategy. This section will guide you through the process of creating an effective launch timeline and marketing strategy that will set the stage for your business's success.

Creating Your Launch Timeline

A launch timeline is essential for organizing your activities leading up to the official opening of your business. Here's how to create one:

1. **Identify Key Milestones:** Start by listing important milestones that need to be achieved before your launch. These may include:

   - Finalizing your business plan

   - Obtaining necessary licenses and permits

   - Setting up your website and social media profiles

   - Hiring staff

   - Launching marketing campaigns

   - Hosting a soft launch event

2. **Set Deadlines:** Assign realistic deadlines to each milestone. Consider using tools like Gantt charts or project management software to visualize your timeline.

3. **Plan for Contingencies:** Always have a backup plan. Delays can happen, so build some buffer time into your timeline to accommodate unexpected challenges.

Example Timeline:

Here's a sample timeline for a three-month launch period:

- Month 1:
  - Finalize business plan (Week 1)
  - Register business name and obtain licenses (Weeks 2-3)
  - Begin hiring process (Weeks 3-4)

- Month 2:
  - Set up website and social media profiles (Weeks 1-2)
  - Develop marketing materials (Weeks 2-3)
  - Launch pre-opening marketing campaign (Week 4)

- Month 3:
  - Conduct soft launch (Week 1)
  - Gather feedback and make adjustments (Weeks 2-3)
  - Official launch event (Week 4)

Developing Your Marketing Strategy

Your marketing strategy is crucial for attracting clients and generating buzz around your new business. Here are key components to consider:

1. **Define Your Unique Selling Proposition (USP):** Identify what sets your Party Planning Business apart from competitors. This could be your unique style, specialized services (like eco-friendly events), or exceptional customer service.

2. **Identify Your Target Audience:** Use the customer personas you created earlier to tailor your marketing messages. Consider demographics, interests, and pain points.

3. **Choose Your Marketing Channels:** Select the most effective channels to reach your audience. Options include:

   - Social media platforms (Instagram, Facebook, Pinterest)

   - Email marketing campaigns

   - Local advertising (flyers, community boards, local magazines)

   - Networking events and trade shows

4. **Create Engaging Content:** Develop content that resonates with your audience. This can include blog posts, videos, and social media updates showcasing your expertise and past events.

5. **Launch Promotions:** Consider offering special promotions or discounts for early clients. This could be a percentage off their first event or complimentary services for referrals.

By carefully planning your launch timeline and developing a solid marketing strategy, you will lay the groundwork for a successful launch and a thriving Party Planning Business. Remember, flexibility and adaptability are key as you navigate the exciting journey ahead!

Visit **www.BusinessBookstore.com/start** to download blank forms, etc.

Activity: Business Launch Checklist

Congratulations on reaching the final stage of preparing for your business launch! This checklist will serve as a comprehensive guide to ensure that you have covered all the essential tasks and considerations before launching your small business. Take your time to review each item and check them off as you complete them.

1. **Legal and Administrative Tasks:**

   ☐ Register your business entity and obtain necessary licenses and permits.

   ☐ Secure your business name and domain.

   ☐ Set up your business bank account and obtain necessary insurance coverage.

   ☐ Complete any required tax registrations and filings.

2. **Brand and Marketing:**

   ☐ Finalize your brand identity, including your logo, colors, and brand messaging.

   ☐ Develop a marketing plan and strategy for your launch, including social media, email marketing, and promotional activities.

   ☐ Create marketing collateral such as website content, social media posts, and promotional materials.

   ☐ Ensure your website is live and optimized for search engines.

3. Product/Service Readiness:

☐ Ensure your product/service is fully developed, tested, and ready for launch.

☐ Set pricing and packaging for your offerings.

☐ Create product/service documentation or instructions for customers, if applicable.

4. Operations and Infrastructure:

☐ Set up your physical location or office space, if applicable.

☐ Establish inventory management systems and procure necessary supplies or equipment.

☐ Implement technology systems and tools to support your operations and customer service.

5. Team and Training:

☐ Hire and train your team members, ensuring they are prepared for the launch.

☐ Communicate roles, responsibilities, and expectations to your team members.

☐ Conduct any necessary team meetings or training sessions to align everyone with the launch plan.

6. Launch Planning and Execution:

☐ Develop a detailed launch timeline with key milestones and deadlines.

☐ Execute your marketing strategy and promotional activities according to the timeline.

☐ Monitor the progress of your launch plan and make adjustments as needed.

7. **Customer Experience and Support:**

 ☐ Prepare to provide excellent customer service and support to new customers.

 ☐ Set up channels for customer inquiries, feedback, and support requests.

 ☐ Train your team members on how to handle customer inquiries and resolve issues effectively.

8. **Post-Launch Evaluation:**

 ☐ Plan to evaluate the success of your launch and gather feedback from customers.

 ☐ Analyze key metrics and performance indicators to assess the effectiveness of your launch strategy.

 ☐ Identify areas for improvement and make adjustments to your business strategy as needed.

Congratulations once again on reaching this exciting milestone in your entrepreneurial journey! By completing this checklist and launching your small business with careful planning and execution, you are setting yourself up for success in the competitive marketplace.

Promote Your Business

Chapter 17
Craft Your Branding Strategy

Key Takeaways

- Defining Brand Identity and Values

- Creating Brand Messaging and Visuals

- Activity: Branding Strategy Workbook

Welcome to Chapter 17: Craft Your Branding Strategy! As a small business owner, you have the unique opportunity to create a brand that resonates with your target audience and sets you apart from the competition. A strong branding strategy is essential for establishing your identity in the marketplace and building lasting relationships with your customers. It's not just about having a catchy logo or a memorable tagline; it's about conveying your values, mission, and the essence of what you offer.

Your brand is the story you tell the world about who you are and what you stand for. It encompasses the emotions, perceptions, and experiences that customers associate with your business. In this chapter, we will delve into the key components of branding and how to effectively communicate your brand identity.

Here are some important aspects we will cover:

- **Defining Your Brand Identity:** Understand the core values and mission that drive your business.

- **Creating Brand Messaging:** Develop a consistent message that resonates with your audience.

- **Visual Branding:** Explore the importance of design elements like logos, colors, and typography in shaping perceptions.

By the end of this chapter, you will have the tools and insights needed to craft a compelling branding strategy that not only attracts customers but also fosters loyalty and trust. Remember, your brand is your business's most valuable asset—investing time and effort into it will pay off in the long run. Let's get started on building a brand that truly reflects your passion and vision!

Defining Brand Identity and Values

Defining your brand identity and values is a crucial step in establishing a successful Party Planning Business. Your brand identity encompasses how you present your business to the world, while your brand values reflect the principles and beliefs that guide your operations. Together, they help differentiate your business from competitors and create a connection with your target audience.

1. **Understand Your Unique Selling Proposition (USP)**: Your USP is what sets your Party Planning Business apart from others. Consider what makes your services unique. Do you specialize in eco-friendly events, luxury parties, or perhaps themed children's birthdays? Identifying your USP will help to shape your brand identity. For instance, if you focus on sustainable events, your branding may incorporate earthy colors and natural materials.

2. **Define Your Brand Values**: Your brand values are the core principles that drive your business decisions and behavior. They should resonate with your target audience and reflect what you stand for. Here are some common brand values you might consider:

   - **Creativity:** Emphasizing innovative ideas and unique themes for each event.

   - **Customer Focus:** Prioritizing client satisfaction and personalized service.

   - **Integrity:** Being honest and transparent in all dealings.

   - **Sustainability:** Committing to environmentally friendly practices.

Choose 3-5 values that genuinely represent your business philosophy. For example, if you choose "creativity," your marketing materials and event designs should reflect that through vibrant visuals and imaginative concepts.

3. **Create a Brand Story**: Your brand story is a narrative that conveys who you are, what you do, and why you do it. It should evoke emotions and connect with your audience on a personal level. Consider the following elements when crafting your story:

   - **Your Background:** Share your journey into the party planning industry. What inspired you to start this business?

   - **Challenges Overcome:** Discuss any obstacles you faced and how they shaped your values and approach.

   - **Vision for the Future:** Outline your aspirations for your business and the impact you wish to have on your clients.

For example, if you started your business to bring joy to families through memorable celebrations, weave that passion into your story to resonate with potential clients.

4. **Visual Identity**: Your visual identity includes your logo, color palette, typography, and overall design aesthetic. These elements should reflect your brand values and appeal to your target audience. Consider the following:

   - **Logo:** Create a logo that embodies your brand's essence. A playful logo may suit a children's party planner, while a sleek design might appeal to corporate clients.

   - **Color Palette:** Choose colors that evoke the emotions you want associated with your brand. Soft pastels may convey elegance, while bright colors can suggest fun and excitement.

   - **Typography:** Select fonts that align with your brand's personality. A whimsical font can enhance a playful brand, while a clean, modern font may suit a professional image.

5. **Consistency is Key**: Once you have defined your brand identity and values, ensure consistency across all platforms. This includes your website, social media profiles, marketing materials, and client interactions. Consistency helps to build trust and recognition, making it easier for clients to remember and choose your services.

In summary, defining your brand identity and values is a foundational step in establishing your Party Planning Business. By understanding your USP, articulating your brand values, crafting a compelling brand story, creating a cohesive visual identity, and maintaining consistency, you will set a strong foundation for your business's success.

Creating Brand Messaging and Visuals

Creating effective brand messaging and visuals is essential for establishing a strong identity in the Party Planning Business. Your brand messaging communicates who you are, what you stand for, and how you connect with your audience. Visuals, on the other hand, help convey your brand's personality and values through design elements. Together, they create a cohesive brand experience that resonates with potential clients.

1. **Define Your Brand Messaging**: Your brand messaging should reflect your mission, vision, and unique selling proposition (USP). Consider the following steps to develop your messaging:

    - **Identify Your Core Values:** What principles guide your business? For example, if sustainability is a core value, ensure that your messaging emphasizes eco-friendly practices.

    - **Articulate Your Mission Statement:** Write a clear, concise statement that captures the essence of your business. For instance, "We create unforgettable experiences through personalized party planning that brings joy and connection to every event."

    - **Highlight Your Unique Selling Proposition:** What sets you apart from competitors? If you specialize in themed parties or corporate events, make this clear in your messaging.

2. **Develop a Brand Voice**: Your brand voice should reflect your personality and resonate with your target audience. Consider the following aspects:

    - **Tone:** Is your brand voice formal, casual, playful, or professional? For a Party Planning Business, a friendly and approachable tone may be most effective.

    - **Language:** Use language that speaks to your audience. If your target market is young professionals, incorporate trendy phrases or references that appeal to them.

    - **Consistency:** Ensure that your brand voice remains consistent across all platforms, including your website, social media, and marketing materials.

3. **Create Visual Elements**: Visuals play a crucial role in brand recognition. Here are key components to consider:

    - **Logo:** Design a memorable logo that encapsulates your brand identity. It should be versatile enough to work on various platforms, from business cards to social media profiles.

    - **Color Palette:** Choose a color scheme that reflects your brand's personality. For example, vibrant colors may convey fun and excitement, while muted tones could suggest elegance and sophistication.

    - **Typography:** Select fonts that align with your brand voice. A playful script font may work well for a whimsical Party Planning Business, while a clean sans-serif font might suit a more corporate-focused approach.

4. **Create Brand Guidelines**: Documenting your brand messaging and visual elements in a brand guideline can help maintain consistency as your business grows. Include information on:

- Logo usage and variations

- Color codes for digital and print

- Fonts and their applications

- Examples of brand voice in messaging

By carefully crafting your brand messaging and visuals, you'll create a strong foundation for your Party Planning Business. This cohesive identity will not only attract clients but also foster loyalty and trust, essential elements for long-term success.

Visit **www.BusinessBookstore.com/start** to download blank forms, etc.

Activity: Branding Strategy Workbook

The Branding Strategy Workbook will guide you through the process of defining your brand identity, crafting compelling messaging, and designing visual elements that reflect your brand's essence. By completing this workbook, you'll create a roadmap for building a strong and cohesive brand that resonates with your audience.

Instructions:

1. **Brand Identity:**

   - Define your brand's vision, mission, and values.

     _____

     _____

     _____

   - Describe your brand personality and tone of voice.

     _____

     _____

     _____

   - Identify key attributes that differentiate your brand from competitors.

     _____

     _____

     _____

2. **Brand Messaging:**

- Craft your brand story, including its origins and aspirations.

  _____

  _____

  _____

- Define your value proposition and key messaging points.

  _____

  _____

  _____

- Develop taglines, slogans, or key phrases that encapsulate your brand essence.

  _____

  _____

  _____

3. **Visual Elements:**

☐ Design your logo, considering color, typography, and iconography.

☐ Choose a color palette and typography that align with your brand personality.

☐ Select imagery and visual style that reinforce your brand identity and messaging.

4. **Consistency and Guidelines:**

☐ Design your logo, considering color, typography, and iconography.

☐ Choose a color palette and typography that align with your brand personality.

☐ Select imagery and visual style that reinforce your brand identity and messaging.

Brand Strategy Workbook Checklist:

☐ Define brand vision, mission, and values.

☐ Describe brand personality and tone of voice.

☐ Identify key brand attributes and differentiation factors.

☐ Craft brand story and value proposition.

☐ Develop taglines or key messaging points.

☐ Design logo and visual elements.

☐ Choose color palette and typography.

☐ Select imagery and visual style.

☐ Create brand guidelines for consistency.

☐ Review and refine branding strategy.

Conclusion:

Completing the Branding Strategy Workbook is a significant step towards building a strong and memorable brand for your business. Once you've filled out each section, you'll have a comprehensive blueprint that guides your brand's development and ensures consistency in messaging and visual representation. Let's unleash the full potential of your brand and make a lasting impression on your audience!

Chapter 18

Design Your Marketing Strategy

Key Takeaways

- Defining Target Markets and Objectives

- Developing Marketing Mix

- Activity: Marketing Plan Template

Welcome to Chapter 18: Design Your Marketing Strategy! As a small business owner venturing into the exciting world of party planning, developing a solid marketing strategy is crucial for your success. In today's competitive landscape, effective marketing is not just an option; it is a necessity. This chapter will empower you to create a tailored marketing strategy that resonates with your target audience and showcases your unique offerings.

Marketing is more than just promoting your services; it's about building relationships and engaging with your clients. A well-designed marketing strategy helps you identify your target markets, set clear objectives, and determine the best channels to reach your audience. By understanding your audience's needs and preferences, you can craft messages that not only attract attention but also foster loyalty.

Throughout this chapter, you will learn how to:

- Define your target markets and their specific needs.

- Develop a comprehensive marketing mix that includes product, price, place, and promotion.

- Create actionable marketing plans that align with your business goals.

Remember, the key to a successful marketing strategy lies in experimentation and adaptation. What works for one business may not work for another, so be open to trying new approaches and refining your tactics over time. With the right strategy in place, you will not only attract new clients but also create lasting relationships that will help your business thrive.

Let's dive in and start designing a marketing strategy that will set your Party Planning Business on the path to success!

Defining Target Markets and Objectives

Defining your target markets and objectives is a critical step in crafting an effective marketing strategy for your Party Planning Business. Understanding who your ideal customers are and what you want to achieve with your marketing efforts will guide your decisions and help you allocate resources more efficiently.

1. **Identifying Target Markets**: Your target market consists of the specific group of people who are most likely to use your party planning services. To define your target markets, consider the following factors:

   - **Demographics:** Analyze age, gender, income level, education, and occupation. For example, if you specialize in children's parties, your target market may include parents aged 25-40 with disposable income.

   - **Geographics:** Determine the geographical area where you will provide services. Are you focusing on local clients, or do you plan to serve a broader region? For instance, a business based in a metropolitan area may cater to urban clients, while a rural-based planner might target small-town events.

   - **Psychographics:** Explore the interests, values, lifestyles, and behaviors of your potential clients. For example, eco-conscious consumers may be attracted to sustainable event planning services.

   - **Behavioral Factors:** Consider purchasing behavior, brand loyalty, and usage rates. Understanding whether your clients prefer luxury events or budget-friendly options can help you tailor your services accordingly.

To further refine your target market, create customer personas that represent your ideal clients. This can include details such as their age, profession, interests, and challenges they face when planning events. For example, a persona might be "Sarah, a 30-year-old event planner who values creativity and sustainability, looking to host a memorable birthday party for her daughter."

2. **Setting Marketing Objectives**: Once you have a clear understanding of your target markets, it's essential to set specific marketing objectives that align with your overall business goals. Your objectives should be SMART: Specific, Measurable, Achievable, Relevant, and Time-bound. Here are some examples:

- **Increase Brand Awareness:** Aim to reach 1,000 followers on social media platforms within six months.

- **Generate Leads:** Set a goal to acquire 50 new client inquiries per month through your website and social media channels.

- **Boost Sales:** Target a 20% increase in revenue within the next year by launching a new service package.

- **Enhance Customer Retention:** Aim to improve customer loyalty by increasing repeat bookings by 15% over the next year.

When setting objectives, consider the resources available to you and the time frame for achieving these goals. Regularly review and adjust your objectives as needed based on your business performance and market conditions.

In summary, defining your target markets and setting clear marketing objectives will provide a solid foundation for your marketing strategy. By understanding who your customers are and what you want to achieve, you can create targeted campaigns that resonate with your audience and drive your Party Planning Business toward success.

Developing Marketing Mix

The marketing mix is a foundational concept in marketing that helps businesses strategically position their products or services in the market. It consists of four main elements: Product, Price, Place, and Promotion, often referred to as the "4 Ps." Each element plays a crucial role in how you reach and engage your target audience. Understanding and effectively managing these components will enhance your Party Planning Business's ability to attract and retain clients.

1. **Product:** In the context of a Party Planning Business, your product is not just the physical items you provide (like decorations, catering, or entertainment), but also the overall service experience you offer. Consider the following:

    -   **Service Packages:** Offer different tiers of service packages (e.g., basic, premium, and deluxe) that cater to various budgets and needs. For instance, a basic package might include venue selection and basic decor, while a deluxe package could encompass full event coordination, catering, and entertainment.

    -   **Customization:** Allow clients to personalize their events. For example, you could offer customizable themes or color schemes that align with the client's vision.

    -   **Value-Added Services:** Consider additional services such as event consultation, vendor management, or post-event clean-up to enhance your product offering.

2. **Price:** Pricing strategy is vital for attracting clients while ensuring profitability. Here are some considerations:

    *   **Competitive Pricing:** Research competitors' pricing to ensure your rates are competitive. If you offer unique services or exceptional quality, you might justify higher prices.

    *   **Discounts and Promotions:** Implement seasonal promotions or discounts for early bookings to incentivize clients. For example, offering a 10% discount for events booked three months in advance can encourage early commitments.

    *   **Flexible Payment Options:** Consider offering flexible payment plans or deposits to make your services more accessible to a broader audience.

3. **Place:** This refers to how your services are delivered and where clients can access them. In party planning, this can include:

    *   **Online Presence:** Ensure your website is user-friendly and showcases your services clearly. Include an easy-to-navigate portfolio of past events, client testimonials, and a blog with planning tips.

    *   **Networking:** Build relationships with local venues, caterers, and other vendors. A strong network can enhance your service offerings and provide clients with comprehensive solutions.

    *   **Social Media:** Utilize social media platforms to showcase your events and engage with potential clients. Platforms like Instagram and Pinterest are particularly effective for visual storytelling in event planning.

4. **Promotion:** Promoting your services effectively is essential to reach your target audience. Consider these strategies:

    • **Content Marketing:** Create valuable content that addresses common questions or challenges in party planning. This could include blog posts, videos, or downloadable guides.

    • **Email Marketing:** Build an email list and send regular newsletters with tips, success stories, and special offers to keep your audience engaged.

    • **Networking Events:** Attend local business expos, wedding fairs, or community events to showcase your services and connect with potential clients.

In summary, developing a solid marketing mix is essential for the success of your Party Planning Business. By thoughtfully considering each of the 4 Ps—Product, Price, Place, and Promotion—you can create a compelling value proposition that resonates with your target audience and sets your business apart in a competitive market.

Visit **www.BusinessBookstore.com/start** to download blank forms, etc.

Activity: Marketing Plan Template

As you embark on developing your marketing plan, use the following template to organize your thoughts, strategies, and action steps. This template will guide you through key components of your marketing plan, ensuring that you address essential aspects of your marketing strategy.

1. **Executive Summary:**

   - Brief overview of your business and its marketing goals.

   - Summary of key strategies and tactics outlined in the marketing plan.

2. **Business Overview:**

   - Description of your business, its mission, and target market.

   - Analysis of your business's strengths, weaknesses, opportunities, and threats (SWOT).

3. **Market Analysis:**

   - Overview of the industry and market trends.

   - Analysis of target market demographics, psychographics, and buying behavior.

   - Assessment of competitors and their strategies.

4. **Marketing Objectives:**

   - Clear and measurable objectives aligned with overall business goals.

   - Specific targets for increasing brand awareness, acquiring customers, generating leads, etc.

5. **Marketing Strategy:**

- Product positioning and differentiation strategy.

- Pricing strategy and value proposition.

- Distribution channels and logistics.

- Promotional mix, including advertising, public relations, sales promotions, and digital marketing.

6. **Marketing Tactics:**

- Detailed action plans for implementing marketing strategies.

- Specific tactics for each element of the marketing mix.

- Timeline for execution and deadlines for key milestones.

7. **Budget Allocation:**

- Allocation of financial resources to different marketing activities.

- Breakdown of costs for advertising, promotions, events, etc.

8. **Implementation Plan:**

- Assignment of responsibilities to team members or external partners.

- Schedule for executing marketing activities.

- Monitoring and evaluation process to track progress and make adjustments as needed.

9. **Measurement and Analytics:**

- Key performance indicators (KPIs) to measure the effectiveness of marketing efforts.

- Tools and methods for tracking and analyzing performance data.

- Plans for reporting and reviewing results regularly.

10. **Contingency Plan:**

- Anticipated challenges or risks and strategies to mitigate them.

- Backup plans in case of unforeseen circumstances affecting marketing activities.

Instructions:

1. Review each section of the marketing plan template carefully.

2. Fill in the relevant details and information based on your business's unique characteristics, goals, and market environment.

3. Ensure consistency and coherence across all sections to maintain a cohesive marketing strategy.

4. Regularly revisit and update your marketing plan as needed to adapt to changes in the market or business environment.

By completing this Marketing Plan Template, you'll have a comprehensive roadmap to guide your marketing efforts effectively and achieve your business objectives.

Chapter 19

Establish Your Online Presence

Key Takeaways

- Building a Professional Website

- Creating Engaging Social Media Profiles

- Activity: Website Checklist

In today's digital age, establishing a robust online presence is not just an option; it's a necessity for small business owners looking to thrive. Your online presence serves as the foundation for your brand, allowing you to connect with potential clients, showcase your services, and build lasting relationships. As a Party Planning Business, your ability to engage with customers online can significantly impact your success.

Creating a professional website and engaging social media profiles will help you reach a broader audience and elevate your brand's visibility. This chapter will guide you through the essential steps to establish your online presence effectively. You'll learn how to:

- Build a user-friendly and visually appealing website that reflects your brand identity.

- Create engaging social media profiles that resonate with your target audience.

- Utilize online tools and resources to enhance your marketing efforts.

By investing time and effort into your online presence, you will not only attract new clients but also foster trust and credibility within your community. Remember, your website is often the first point of contact for potential customers, so making a positive impression is crucial.

As you embark on this journey, keep in mind that establishing your online presence is an ongoing process. Regular updates, engaging content, and interaction with your audience are key to maintaining relevance in the ever-evolving digital landscape. Let's dive in and explore how you can effectively establish and enhance your online presence, paving the way for your Party Planning Business to shine!

Building a Professional Website

In today's digital age, having a professional website is essential for any Party Planning Business. Your website serves as your online storefront, showcasing your services, portfolio, and contact information to potential clients. Here are key elements to consider when building a professional website:

1. **Choose the Right Platform:** Selecting a user-friendly website builder is crucial. Popular options include:

   - **Wix:** Offers drag-and-drop functionality and customizable templates.

   - **Squarespace:** Known for its visually stunning designs and ease of use.

   - **WordPress:** Highly customizable and ideal for those who want more control over their website.

2. **Define Your Brand Identity:** Your website should reflect your brand identity. Use consistent colors, fonts, and logos throughout the site. This helps establish brand recognition and trust. For example, if your brand is vibrant and fun, use bright colors and playful fonts. Conversely, if your brand is more elegant, opt for a sophisticated color palette and classic typography.

3. **Create a User-Friendly Layout:** Ensure that your website is easy to navigate. Here are some tips:

   - Use clear headings and subheadings to guide visitors.

   - Include a search bar for easy access to information.

   - Limit the number of menu items to avoid overwhelming visitors.

4. **Showcase Your Services:** Clearly outline the services you offer. Consider creating dedicated pages for different offerings, such as:

    - **Event Planning:** Describe your planning process and types of events you handle.

    - **Decor Rentals:** Showcase available decor items with high-quality images.

    - **Consultations:** Detail the consultation process and what clients can expect.

5. **Include a Portfolio:** Potential clients want to see your work. Create a portfolio section that highlights your past events. Include:

    - High-resolution images of events you've planned.

    - Client testimonials to build credibility.

    - Descriptions of the events, including challenges and how you overcame them.

6. **Optimize for SEO:** Search Engine Optimization (SEO) helps your website rank higher in search results, making it easier for potential clients to find you. Here are some basic SEO practices:

    - Use relevant keywords throughout your website content.

    - Optimize image alt tags with descriptive text.

    - Ensure your website loads quickly and is mobile-friendly.

7. **Include Contact Information:** Make it easy for clients to reach you. Include a dedicated contact page with:

    - Your phone number and email address.

    - A contact form for inquiries.

    - Links to your social media profiles.

8. **Regularly Update Your Content:** Keep your website fresh and engaging by regularly updating your content. Consider adding a blog to share tips, trends, and insights related to party planning. This not only provides value to your visitors but also enhances your SEO efforts.

By following these guidelines, you can create a professional website that effectively represents your Party Planning Business and attracts potential clients. Remember, your website is often the first impression clients will have of your business, so invest the time and effort to make it shine.

Creating Engaging Social Media Profiles

Creating engaging social media profiles is a crucial step in establishing your Party Planning Business's online presence. Your social media profiles are often the first impression potential clients will have of your brand, so it's essential to make them visually appealing and informative. Here are some key elements to consider when crafting your profiles:

- **Profile Picture:** Choose a professional and recognizable profile picture. This could be your business logo or a high-quality image of you if you are the face of the brand. Ensure that it is clear and represents your business identity.

- **Cover Photo:** Utilize the cover photo space effectively to showcase your work. This could be a collage of your past events or a captivating image that reflects your brand's style. Make sure it is visually appealing and aligns with the overall aesthetic of your business.

- **Bio/Description:** Write a concise and engaging bio that clearly describes what your business does. Use keywords that potential clients might search for. For example, "Specializing in creating unforgettable birthday parties, weddings, and corporate events. Let us bring your vision to life!"

- **Contact Information:** Make it easy for potential clients to reach you. Include your email address, phone number, and website link. This information should be easily accessible and prominently displayed on your profile.

- **Call to Action:** Incorporate a call to action (CTA) in your bio. This could be an invitation to visit your website, book a consultation, or follow your page for tips and inspiration. For example, "Follow us for party planning tips and ideas!"

- **Highlight Your Services:** Use the highlights feature available on platforms like Instagram to showcase your services, testimonials, and past events. This gives visitors a quick overview of what you offer and builds credibility.

- **Consistent Branding:** Ensure that your profiles reflect consistent branding across all platforms. Use the same color scheme, logo, and tone of voice. This helps in building brand recognition and trust.

Once your profile is set up, it's important to keep it active and engaging. Here are some tips to maintain your social media presence:

- **Regular Posting:** Create a content calendar to plan your posts in advance. Aim for a mix of promotional content, behind-the-scenes glimpses, client testimonials, and tips related to party planning.

- **Engagement:** Interact with your audience by responding to comments and messages promptly. Ask questions in your posts to encourage engagement and create a sense of community.

- **Visual Content:** Use high-quality images and videos to showcase your events. Visual content is more likely to be shared and can significantly increase your reach.

- **Utilize Hashtags:** Research and include relevant hashtags in your posts to increase visibility. This can help potential clients discover your business when searching for party planning services.

- **Collaborate:** Partner with other local businesses or influencers in your niche to expand your reach. This could involve hosting joint events or giveaways, which can attract new followers and potential clients.

In summary, creating engaging social media profiles is essential for your Party Planning Business. By focusing on visual appeal, clear communication, and consistent branding, you can attract potential clients and establish a strong online presence. Remember to keep your profiles active and engaging to foster relationships with your audience.

Activity: Website Checklist

Before launching your website, it's important to ensure that it meets certain standards and includes essential elements to provide a positive user experience and effectively showcase your brand. Use the following checklist to review your website and make any necessary adjustments:

> Visit **www.BusinessHelpStore.com** to search for your business domain.

1. **Domain Name:**

   ☐ Domain name is relevant to your business.

   ☐ Domain name is easy to spell and remember.

   ☐ Domain is registered and active.

2. **Hosting:**

   ☐ Website is hosted on a reliable server.

   ☐ Hosting plan provides adequate bandwidth and storage.

3. **Design and Layout:**

   ☐ Website design is visually appealing and consistent with your brand identity.
   ☐ Layout is user-friendly and easy to navigate.

   ☐ Mobile responsiveness: Website is optimized for mobile devices and displays properly on various screen sizes.

4. **Content:**

☐ All content is clear, concise, and error-free.

☐ Contact information (phone number, email address, physical address) is prominently displayed.

☐ About Us page provides information about your business, mission, and values.

☐ Product or service pages include detailed descriptions, pricing, and images.

☐ Testimonials or customer reviews are showcased to build credibility.

5. **Navigation:**

☐ Navigation menu is easy to find and navigate.

☐ Website has a logical hierarchy with clearly defined categories and subcategories.

☐ Internal links are used to guide users to relevant pages within the website.

6. **SEO Optimization:**

☐ Meta titles and descriptions are optimized with relevant keywords.

☐ Image alt text is used to describe images for improved accessibility and SEO.

☐ Website content is optimized for search engines to improve visibility and rankings.

7. **Security:**

☐ Website has an SSL certificate installed to encrypt data and secure online transactions.

☐ Backup system is in place to protect against data loss or website downtime.

8. **Functionality:**

☐ Forms (contact forms, signup forms, etc.) are functional and submit data correctly.

☐ Links and buttons are working properly and lead to the intended destinations.

☐ E-commerce functionality (if applicable) is fully operational, including shopping cart, checkout process, and payment gateway integration.

9. **Legal Compliance:**

☐ Privacy policy is in place and accessible to users.

☐ Terms and conditions are provided for website visitors.

☐ Website complies with relevant laws and regulations, such as GDPR or CCPA (if applicable).

10. **Analytics and Tracking:**

☐ Website analytics tool (such as Google Analytics) is installed to track website traffic, user behavior, and other key metrics.

☐ Conversion tracking is set up to monitor the performance of marketing campaigns and goals.

Once you have completed the items on this checklist and made any necessary adjustments, your website will be ready to launch and effectively represent your business online.

Chapter 20
Implement Social Media Marketing

Key Takeaways

- Choosing Social Media Platforms

- Creating Content and Engagement Strategies

- Activity: Social Media Strategy Planner

Welcome to Chapter 20: Implement Social Media Marketing! In today's digital age, social media has become an indispensable tool for small business owners looking to connect with their audience, build brand awareness, and drive sales. Whether you are just starting your Party Planning Business or seeking to enhance your existing marketing efforts, harnessing the power of social media can significantly elevate your business presence.

As a small business owner, you have a unique advantage. You can engage with your customers on a personal level, share your passion for party planning, and showcase your creativity in ways that larger companies often cannot. Social media platforms provide an opportunity to tell your story, share your expertise, and build a community around your brand. By leveraging these platforms effectively, you can create meaningful connections that foster loyalty and encourage referrals.

In this chapter, we will explore:

- Choosing the right social media platforms for your business

- Creating engaging content that resonates with your target audience

- Developing strategies to increase engagement and grow your following

Remember, social media marketing is not just about promoting your services; it's about building relationships. By sharing valuable content, responding to inquiries, and participating in conversations, you can position yourself as a trusted expert in the party planning industry. As you embark on this journey, embrace the learning process and be open to experimenting with different strategies. Your efforts will not only enhance your business visibility but also create a vibrant community around your brand.

Let's dive in and discover how to make social media a powerful ally in your Party Planning Business!

Choosing Social Media Platforms

Choosing the right social media platforms for your Party Planning Business is crucial for effectively reaching your target audience and maximizing your marketing efforts. Each platform has its unique characteristics, demographics, and strengths, making it essential to select those that align with your business goals and customer preferences. Here are some key considerations to help you make informed decisions:

1. **Understand Your Audience:** Before diving into platform selection, take the time to analyze your target audience. Consider their age, interests, and online behavior. For example:

   - **Facebook:** This platform is popular among a wide age range, making it suitable for family-oriented events, weddings, and community gatherings.

   - **Instagram:** With its focus on visuals, Instagram is ideal for showcasing stunning event photos, decor ideas, and behind-the-scenes content, appealing to younger audiences.

   - **Pinterest:** A go-to platform for event inspiration, Pinterest attracts users looking for ideas for weddings, parties, and DIY projects, making it a valuable tool for sharing your portfolio.

2. **Define Your Content Strategy:** Consider the type of content you plan to create and share. Different platforms support various content formats:

   - **Facebook:** Great for longer posts, event promotions, and community engagement through groups.

   - **Instagram:** Focus on high-quality images and short videos. Utilize Stories and Reels to engage your audience in a more dynamic way.

   - **Twitter/X:** Best for quick updates, sharing industry news, and engaging in conversations with clients and other professionals.

- **LinkedIn:** Ideal for networking with other businesses and professionals in the event planning industry.

3. **Evaluate Your Resources:** Consider the time and resources you have available for managing your social media presence. Each platform requires different levels of engagement:

  - **Facebook and Instagram:** These platforms require regular posting and interaction with followers to build a loyal community.

  - **Pinterest:** Once you create and pin content, it can continue to drive traffic over time with less frequent updates.

  - **Twitter/X:** Requires constant engagement due to its fast-paced nature; you may need to post multiple times a day.

4. **Analyze Competitors:** Research what platforms your competitors are using and how they engage their audience. This can provide insights into effective strategies and help you identify gaps in their approach that you can capitalize on.

5. **Test and Adapt:** Don't be afraid to experiment with different platforms. Start by establishing a presence on a few key networks, then analyze the results. Use analytics tools to track engagement, follower growth, and conversion rates. Based on this data, you can adapt your strategy and focus on the platforms that yield the best results.

In conclusion, choosing the right social media platforms for your Party Planning Business involves understanding your audience, defining your content strategy, evaluating your resources, analyzing competitors, and being willing to test and adapt. By strategically selecting platforms that align with your business goals, you can effectively engage with your audience and promote your services.

Creating Content and Engagement Strategies

In today's digital landscape, creating engaging content is crucial for your Party Planning Business. It not only helps attract potential clients but also builds your brand's reputation and fosters customer loyalty. This section will guide you through effective content creation and engagement strategies tailored for your audience.

1. **Understand Your Audience**: Before creating content, it's essential to understand who your audience is. Conduct surveys or use analytics tools to gather information about their preferences, interests, and pain points. This data will inform your content strategy, ensuring that your material resonates with your target market.

2. **Types of Content to Create**: Consider diversifying your content types to keep your audience engaged. Here are some suggestions:

   - **Blog Posts:** Write informative articles about party planning tips, trends, and themes. For example, a post titled "Top 10 Unique Themes for Your Next Birthday Party" can attract readers looking for inspiration.

   - **How-To Guides:** Create step-by-step guides for specific aspects of party planning, such as "How to Choose the Perfect Venue" or "DIY Party Decorations on a Budget."

   - **Videos:** Produce short videos showcasing your event setups, behind-the-scenes processes, or client testimonials. Platforms like YouTube and Instagram are ideal for sharing video content.

   - **Infographics:** Design visually appealing infographics that summarize key information, such as budgeting tips or a checklist for planning a successful event.

   - **Social Media Posts:** Share engaging images and updates on platforms like Instagram, Facebook, and Pinterest. Use captivating captions and hashtags to increase visibility.

3. **Content Distribution Channels**: Once you've created your content, it's time to share it effectively. Here are some channels to consider:

    *   **Your Website:** Host a blog or resource section on your website where visitors can access your content easily.

    *   **Social Media:** Share your content across various social media platforms. Tailor your posts to fit the style and audience of each platform.

    *   **Email Newsletters:** Build an email list and send regular newsletters featuring your latest content, promotions, and event highlights. This keeps your audience engaged and informed.

    *   **Collaborations:** Partner with other businesses or influencers in the event planning industry to reach a broader audience. Guest blogging or co-hosting events can be beneficial.

4. **Engagement Strategies**: Creating content is just the first step; engaging with your audience is equally important. Here are some strategies to foster engagement:

    *   **Encourage Comments:** Ask questions at the end of your blog posts or social media updates to invite discussions. Respond to comments to build a community.

    *   **Run Contests or Giveaways:** Organize contests that require participants to share your content or tag friends. This increases your visibility and encourages participation.

    *   **Create Polls and Surveys:** Use tools like Instagram Stories or Facebook polls to gather opinions on topics relevant to your audience. This not only engages them but also provides valuable insights.

    *   **Host Live Q&A Sessions:** Utilize platforms like Facebook Live or Instagram Live to answer questions from your audience in real-time. This interaction can enhance your credibility and build trust.

By implementing these content creation and engagement strategies, you will not only attract potential clients but also establish a strong online presence for your Party Planning Business. Remember, the key is to be consistent, authentic, and responsive to your audience's needs.

Visit **www.BusinessBookstore.com/start** to download blank forms, etc.

Activity: Social Media Strategy Planner

Congratulations on reaching the stage where you're ready to craft a comprehensive social media strategy for your business! This activity will guide you through the process of developing a strategic plan to effectively leverage social media platforms for your business objectives.

Instructions:

1. **Define Your Goals:** Start by clearly outlining your social media goals. What do you aim to achieve through your social media efforts? Examples include increasing brand awareness, driving website traffic, generating leads, fostering customer engagement, and boosting sales.

2. **Identify Your Target Audience:** Describe your target audience in detail, including demographics, interests, behaviors, and pain points. Understanding your audience will help you tailor your content and messaging to resonate with them effectively.

3. **Choose Social Media Platforms:** Select the social media platforms that align with your target audience and business goals. Consider factors such as platform demographics, user engagement, and content format preferences.

4. **Content Strategy:** Outline the key elements of your content strategy, including content themes, types, frequency, and tone of voice. Determine the topics you'll cover, the formats you'll use, and the posting schedule you'll follow.

5. **Engagement Tactics:** Identify strategies to encourage audience engagement and interaction on social media. This may include asking questions, running polls or contests, responding to comments, and sharing user-generated content.

6. **Content Calendar:** Create a content calendar outlining the timing and frequency of your social media posts. This calendar will help you stay organized, plan ahead, and maintain consistency in your posting schedule.

7. **Monitoring and Analysis:** Establish metrics to measure the success of your social media efforts. Track key performance indicators (KPIs) such as reach, engagement, clicks, conversions, and ROI. Regularly analyze your data to identify trends, insights, and areas for improvement.

8. **Adjustment and Optimization:** Based on your analysis, make adjustments to your social media strategy as needed. Experiment with different tactics, content formats, and posting times to optimize your results and achieve your goals more effectively.

Social Media Strategy Planner:

1. **Goals:**

_____

_____

_____

2. **Target Audience:**

_____

_____

_____

3. **Social Media Platforms:**

_____

_____

_____

4. **Content Strategy:**

  • Content Themes: _____

  • Content Types: _____

  • Posting Frequency: _____

  • Tone of Voice: _____

5. **Engagement Tactics:**

_____

_____

_____

6. **Content Calendar:**

_____

_____

_____

7. **Monitoring and Analysis:**

_____

_____

_____

8. **Adjustment and Optimization:**

_____

_____

_____

By completing this Social Media Strategy Planner, you'll have a clear roadmap for implementing your social media strategy and achieving your business objectives. Remember to regularly review and update your strategy to stay aligned with your evolving business goals and audience preferences.

Date	Platform	Content type	Content Description	Focused Keywords	KPI
Ex. 1/1/24	Facebook	Video	Google my business guide	Google My Business Help	Likes and Views

Chapter 21

Create Content for Your Business

Key Takeaways

- Content Planning and Ideation

- Content Creation and Distribution

- Activity: Content Calendar

Welcome to Chapter 21 of your journey in starting a successful Party Planning Business! In this chapter, we will explore the essential topic of content creation, a powerful tool that can help you connect with your audience, showcase your expertise, and ultimately drive sales. As a small business owner, creating compelling content is not just an option; it's a necessity in today's digital landscape.

Content is the voice of your brand. It allows you to tell your story, share your knowledge, and engage with potential clients in a meaningful way. Whether it's through blog posts, social media updates, or newsletters, every piece of content you create can help build trust and credibility with your audience. Remember, people are more likely to do business with those they know, like, and trust. By providing valuable and informative content, you position yourself as an authority in the party planning industry.

In this chapter, we will cover:

- **Content Planning and Ideation:** Learn how to brainstorm and organize content that resonates with your audience.

- **Content Creation and Distribution:** Discover effective methods for creating high-quality content and how to share it across various platforms.

As you embark on this content creation journey, keep in mind that consistency is key. Regularly publishing content not only keeps your audience engaged but also improves your visibility in search engines. With the right strategies in place, you can turn your content into a powerful marketing tool that elevates your business to new heights. Let's dive in and start crafting content that captivates and converts!

Content Planning and Ideation

Content planning and ideation are crucial components of a successful Party Planning Business. They help you create engaging, relevant, and valuable content that resonates with your target audience. This section will guide you through the process of developing a content plan and generating creative ideas that align with your business goals.

1. **Understanding Your Audience**: Before diving into content planning, it's essential to understand your audience's needs, preferences, and pain points. Conducting audience research can provide insights into what types of content will resonate with them. Consider creating customer personas that outline their demographics, interests, and challenges. This foundational knowledge will inform your content strategy and help you create tailored content that engages your audience.

2. **Setting Content Goals**: Establish clear objectives for your content. What do you want to achieve? Your goals could include:

   - Increasing brand awareness

   - Generating leads

   - Engaging existing customers

   - Establishing authority in the party planning industry

By setting specific, measurable, achievable, relevant, and time-bound (SMART) goals, you can better assess the success of your content efforts.

3. **Content Types and Formats**: There are various types of content you can create for your Party Planning Business. Here are some suggestions:

-   **Blog Posts:** Share tips, trends, and insights related to party planning. For example, you could write about "10 Unique Themes for Birthday Parties" or "How to Choose the Perfect Venue."

-   **Videos:** Create tutorials or behind-the-scenes footage of your events. Video content can be highly engaging and shareable.

-   **Infographics:** Use infographics to present data or tips visually. For example, an infographic on "The Ultimate Party Planning Checklist" can be informative and easy to share.

-   **Social Media Posts:** Regularly post engaging content on platforms like Instagram and Facebook. Share photos from events, client testimonials, or quick tips.

-   **Newsletters:** Send out regular updates to your subscribers with valuable content, upcoming events, or special promotions.

4. **Brainstorming Content Ideas**: Generating content ideas can sometimes feel daunting. Here are some techniques to spark creativity:

-   **Mind Mapping:** Start with a central theme (e.g., party planning) and branch out with related topics, ideas, and formats.

-   **Keyword Research:** Use tools like Google Keyword Planner or Ubersuggest to find popular search terms related to party planning. This can inform your blog topics and social media posts.

-   **Competitor Analysis:** Look at what your competitors are doing. Identify gaps in their content that you can fill or find inspiration from their successful posts.

-   **Customer Feedback:** Ask your audience what topics they would like to learn more about. This can be done through surveys or social media polls.

5. **Creating a Content Calendar**: Once you have a list of content ideas, organize them into a content calendar. This calendar should outline:

    - Content topics

    - Content formats

    - Publication dates

    - Distribution channels

A content calendar helps you stay consistent and ensures a steady flow of content that aligns with your business objectives.

In conclusion, effective content planning and ideation are essential for engaging your audience and promoting your Party Planning Business. By understanding your audience, setting clear goals, exploring various content formats, brainstorming ideas, and creating a content calendar, you can develop a robust content strategy that drives results.

Content Creation and Distribution

Content creation is a vital aspect of any Party Planning Business, as it helps you engage with your audience, showcase your expertise, and promote your services. In this section, we will explore effective strategies for creating compelling content and distributing it to reach your target audience.

1. **Understanding Your Audience**: Before you start creating content, it's essential to understand who your audience is. Consider their interests, preferences, and pain points. For instance, if your target audience consists of parents planning children's birthday parties, you might focus on fun, creative ideas that cater to kids. Conduct surveys or use social media polls to gather insights into what your audience wants to see.

2. **Types of Content to Create**: There are various types of content you can create to engage your audience:

   - **Blog Posts:** Write informative articles that provide tips, trends, and advice related to party planning. For example, "10 Tips for Planning a Stress-Free Wedding" or "Creative Themes for Kids' Birthday Parties."

   - **Videos:** Create short videos showcasing your event setups, DIY projects, or behind-the-scenes footage of your planning process. Platforms like YouTube or Instagram Reels are great for this.

   - **Infographics:** Design visually appealing infographics that summarize key information, such as a checklist for planning a corporate event or a timeline for wedding planning.

   - **Social Media Posts:** Share engaging images, quotes, and tips on platforms like Instagram, Facebook, and Pinterest. Use relevant hashtags to increase visibility.

   - **Newsletters:** Send regular newsletters to your subscribers featuring updates, promotions, and valuable content. This keeps your audience engaged and informed.

3. **Content Creation Process**: To streamline your content creation process, consider the following steps:

    *   **Brainstorm Ideas:** Set aside time to brainstorm content ideas. Use tools like Google Trends or BuzzSumo to identify trending topics in the party planning niche.

    *   **Create a Content Calendar:** Plan your content in advance by creating a content calendar. This helps you stay organized and ensures a consistent flow of content.

    *   **Write and Edit:** Draft your content and revise it for clarity, grammar, and engagement. Consider using tools like Grammarly to help with editing.

    *   **Design Visuals:** Use graphic design tools like Canva to create visuals that complement your content. Eye-catching images can significantly enhance engagement.

4. **Content Distribution Strategies**: Creating great content is only half the battle; you also need to effectively distribute it to reach your audience. Here are some strategies:

    *   **Social Media:** Share your content across various social media platforms. Tailor your posts to each platform's audience and format for maximum impact.

    *   **Email Marketing:** Use your email list to distribute newsletters and promotional content. Personalize your emails for better engagement.

    *   **Collaborate with Influencers:** Partner with influencers or bloggers in the party planning space to reach a broader audience. They can share your content with their followers.

    *   **SEO Optimization:** Optimize your content for search engines by using relevant keywords and phrases. This increases the chances of your content being discovered by potential clients.

By focusing on creating valuable content and distributing it effectively, you can enhance your visibility, build trust with your audience, and ultimately grow your Party Planning Business.

Visit **www.BusinessBookstore.com/start** to download blank forms, etc.

Activity: Content Calendar

Creating a content calendar is a strategic way to plan and organize your content initiatives across various channels. This tool allows you to map out your content strategy, schedule publication dates, and ensure consistency in your messaging. Follow the steps below to create your own content calendar:

1. **Identify Content Themes and Topics:** Start by brainstorming content ideas that align with your business objectives and resonate with your target audience. Consider seasonal trends, industry events, and customer pain points when selecting topics for your content calendar.

2. **Outline Content Formats and Channels:** Determine the types of content you'll create, such as blog posts, videos, infographics, or social media posts. Choose the channels where you'll distribute each piece of content, such as your website, blog, social media platforms, or email newsletters.

3. **Assign Publication Dates:** Use a calendar template to assign publication dates to each piece of content. Consider factors such as content frequency, publishing cadence, and seasonal trends when scheduling your content. Be realistic about your bandwidth and resources when setting publication dates.

4. **Allocate Resources and Responsibilities:** Identify team members or external collaborators responsible for creating, editing, and publishing each piece of content. Clearly define roles and responsibilities to ensure smooth execution and accountability throughout the content creation process.

5. **Incorporate SEO Keywords and Optimization:** Integrate relevant keywords and SEO optimization techniques into your content calendar to enhance the discoverability and search visibility of your content. Align your content topics with keyword research and SEO best practices to attract organic traffic to your website.

6. **Include Promotion and Distribution Strategies:** Plan how you'll promote and distribute your content across various channels to maximize its reach and impact. Incorporate social media promotion, email marketing, paid advertising, and content syndication into your content calendar to amplify your message.

7. **Monitor and Analyze Performance:** Regularly monitor the performance of your content initiatives using analytics tools and metrics such as website traffic, engagement rates, social media metrics, and conversion metrics. Use data-driven insights to optimize your content strategy and refine your content calendar over time.

Conclusion:

By creating a comprehensive content calendar, you can streamline your content planning process, maintain consistency in your messaging, and optimize the effectiveness of your content initiatives. Use the provided template to organize your content strategy and keep track of your content schedule. Remember to adapt and iterate your content calendar based on evolving business needs, audience feedback, and performance insights.

Date	Content Topic	Content Format	Distribution Channel	Responsible Party

Chapter 22

Plan Advertising and Promotions

Key Takeaways

- Budgeting for Advertising Campaigns

- Selecting Advertising Channels and Methods

- Activity: Advertising Campaign Planner

Welcome to Chapter 22: Plan Advertising and Promotions! As a small business owner, you have the unique opportunity to connect with your audience in meaningful ways. Advertising and promotions are not just about selling your services; they are about telling your story, showcasing your creativity, and building lasting relationships with your clients.

In today's competitive marketplace, effective advertising can set you apart from the crowd. It allows you to communicate your brand values, highlight your unique offerings, and attract the right customers. Whether you are planning a grand opening, a seasonal promotion, or a special event, having a well-thought-out advertising strategy is crucial for maximizing your reach and impact.

Throughout this chapter, we will explore various aspects of advertising and promotions, including:

- **Budgeting for Advertising Campaigns:** Learn how to allocate your resources wisely to achieve the best results.

- **Selecting Advertising Channels:** Discover the different platforms available and how to choose the right ones for your target audience.

- **Creating Compelling Campaigns:** Understand the elements of successful advertising that resonate with potential clients.

Remember, advertising is not just about spending money; it's about making smart investments that yield returns. By carefully planning your advertising strategies, you can create buzz around your business, attract new customers, and foster loyalty among existing ones. Let's dive in and empower your business with impactful advertising and promotional tactics that will help you thrive!

Budgeting for Advertising Campaigns

Budgeting for advertising campaigns is a crucial step in ensuring the success of your Party Planning Business. A well-planned budget helps you allocate resources effectively, measure your return on investment (ROI), and make informed decisions about where to invest your marketing dollars. Here's a guide to help you create a comprehensive advertising budget.

1. **Determine Your Overall Marketing Budget**: Before diving into advertising specifics, establish your overall marketing budget. A common rule of thumb is to allocate 5-10% of your expected revenue for marketing. For example, if you anticipate earning $100,000 in your first year, consider setting aside $5,000 to $10,000 for marketing efforts. This amount can be adjusted based on your business goals and market conditions.

2. **Identify Advertising Goals**: Clearly define the goals of your advertising campaigns. Are you aiming to increase brand awareness, generate leads, or drive sales for a specific event? Having clear objectives will guide your budgeting process and help you measure success. For instance, if your goal is to increase brand awareness, you might focus on social media ads and local event sponsorships.

3. **Allocate Funds to Different Advertising Channels**: Once you have a total budget and defined goals, allocate your funds across various advertising channels. Consider the following options:

    *   **Social Media Advertising:** Platforms like Facebook and Instagram allow you to target specific demographics. Depending on your target audience, you might allocate 30-40% of your budget here.

    *   **Google Ads:** Pay-per-click (PPC) advertising can be effective for reaching potential clients actively searching for party planning services. Consider dedicating 20-30% of your budget to this channel.

    *   **Print Advertising:** Local magazines, newspapers, or flyers can reach your community effectively. Allocate 10-15% of your budget for this, especially if you're targeting local events.

    *   **Event Sponsorships:** Partnering with local events can enhance your visibility. Consider setting aside 10-20% of your budget for sponsorship opportunities.

    *   **Email Marketing:** Investing in an email marketing platform can be cost-effective. Allocate around 5-10% of your budget for creating and sending targeted campaigns.

4. **Monitor and Adjust Your Budget**: As your campaigns progress, continuously monitor their performance. Use analytics tools to track engagement, conversions, and ROI. If a particular channel is performing exceptionally well, consider reallocating funds from underperforming areas to maximize your results. For instance, if your social media ads are generating leads at a lower cost per acquisition than Google Ads, shift some of your budget accordingly.

5. **Plan for Contingencies**: Advertising landscapes can change rapidly, so it's wise to set aside a small portion of your budget (around 5-10%) for unexpected opportunities or adjustments. This fund can be used for spontaneous promotions or to capitalize on trends that align with your business.

In summary, budgeting for advertising campaigns requires careful planning and flexibility. By determining your overall marketing budget, setting clear goals, allocating funds wisely, monitoring performance, and planning for contingencies, you can create effective advertising strategies that drive growth for your Party Planning Business.

Selecting Advertising Channels and Methods

Selecting the right advertising channels and methods is crucial for the success of your Party Planning Business. The right mix of channels can help you reach your target audience effectively, maximize your budget, and ultimately drive more clients to your services. Here are some key considerations and options to help you make informed decisions.

1. **Understand Your Target Audience**: Before diving into advertising channels, it's essential to have a clear understanding of your target audience. Consider their demographics, interests, and behaviors. Are they primarily young families, corporate clients, or couples planning weddings? Tailoring your advertising strategy to meet the preferences of your audience will increase your chances of success.

2. **Explore Digital Advertising**: In today's digital age, online advertising is a powerful tool for reaching potential clients. Here are some effective digital advertising methods:

    - **Social Media Advertising:** Platforms like Facebook, Instagram, and Pinterest are ideal for showcasing your party planning services. Use targeted ads to reach specific demographics based on age, location, and interests. For instance, Instagram is particularly effective for visually appealing content, making it perfect for displaying event setups and decorations.

    - **Google Ads:** Pay-per-click (PPC) advertising through Google can help your business appear in search results when potential clients look for party planning services. Use relevant keywords such as "wedding planner" or "corporate event planning" to attract the right audience.

    - **Email Marketing:** Build an email list of past clients and interested individuals. Sending out regular newsletters with tips, event ideas, and special offers can keep your business top-of-mind and encourage referrals.

3. **Utilize Traditional Advertising**: While digital methods are essential, traditional advertising still holds value, especially in local markets. Consider the following:

   - **Print Advertising:** Advertise in local magazines, newspapers, or community bulletins that target your audience. A well-placed ad can attract clients who prefer traditional media.

   - **Networking Events:** Attend local business expos, bridal shows, or community events. Set up a booth or sponsor an event to showcase your services. This face-to-face interaction can lead to valuable connections.

   - **Direct Mail:** Sending postcards or brochures to local residents can be an effective way to promote your services. Highlight special packages or seasonal offerings to grab attention.

4. **Consider Partnerships and Collaborations**: Forming partnerships with other local businesses can amplify your advertising efforts. For example:

   - Collaborate with venues, caterers, or photographers to create joint marketing campaigns. This not only expands your reach but also builds credibility through association.

   - Offer referral discounts to businesses that send clients your way, creating a mutually beneficial relationship.

5. **Measure and Adjust Your Strategy**: Once you have implemented your advertising strategy, it's crucial to track its effectiveness. Use tools like Google Analytics for online campaigns or ask new clients how they heard about you. This data will help you understand what works and what doesn't, allowing you to adjust your approach accordingly.

In conclusion, selecting the right advertising channels and methods requires careful consideration of your target audience and a mix of both digital and traditional strategies. By continuously measuring your efforts and adapting your strategy, you can effectively promote your Party Planning Business and attract more clients.

Visit **www.BusinessBookstore.com/start** to download blank forms, etc.

Activity: Advertising Campaign Planner

Congratulations on taking the next step in planning your advertising campaigns! Use the following checklist to organize and outline your advertising strategy:

☐ **Define Campaign Objectives:** Clearly define the goals and objectives of your advertising campaign, such as increasing brand awareness, driving website traffic, generating leads, or boosting sales.

☐ **Identify Target Audience:** Describe your target audience demographics and psychographics, including age, gender, location, interests, and preferences.

☐ **Determine Advertising Budget:** Set a realistic budget for your advertising campaign based on your business goals, available resources, and the cost of advertising channels and methods.

☐ **Select Advertising Channels:** Choose the most suitable advertising channels and methods to reach your target audience effectively, considering factors such as audience behavior, preferences, and budget constraints.

☐ **Develop Messaging and Creative Assets:** Create compelling ad copy and visual assets that resonate with your target audience and effectively communicate your brand message and value proposition.

☐ **Set Campaign Timeline:** Establish a timeline for your advertising campaign, including start and end dates, as well as key milestones and deadlines for content creation, campaign launch, and performance evaluation.

☐ **Implement Tracking and Measurement:** Set up tracking mechanisms and analytics tools to monitor the performance of your advertising campaign, track key metrics such as impressions, clicks, conversions, and ROI, and measure the effectiveness of your ads.

☐ **Monitor and Optimize Campaign Performance:** Regularly review and analyze campaign performance data to identify trends, strengths, and areas for improvement. Make data-driven decisions to optimize your advertising strategy and maximize results.

☐ **Allocate Resources and Responsibilities:** Assign roles and responsibilities to team members or external partners involved in executing the advertising campaign, ensuring clear communication and accountability.

☐ **Review and Refine Strategy:** Conduct post-campaign analysis to evaluate the overall effectiveness of your advertising strategy, identify lessons learned, and make recommendations for future campaigns.

Conclusion:

Completing this Advertising Campaign Planner will help you organize and execute your advertising campaigns more effectively, leading to better results and ROI for your small business.

Next Steps:

Refer to this checklist regularly throughout the planning and execution of your advertising campaigns, and don't hesitate to make adjustments as needed to optimize your strategy and achieve your business goals.

Chapter 23
Manage Customer Relationships

Key Takeaways

- Implementing Customer Relationship Management Systems

- Providing Excellent Customer Service

- Activity: CRM Implementation Checklist

Welcome to Chapter 23: Manage Customer Relationships! As a small business owner, you understand that your customers are the lifeblood of your Party Planning Business. Building and maintaining strong relationships with your clients not only fosters loyalty but also encourages referrals, which are invaluable for growth. In this chapter, we will explore the significance of effective customer relationship management (CRM) and how it can transform your business.

In today's competitive landscape, exceptional customer service is no longer just an option; it's a necessity. Customers are increasingly discerning and expect personalized experiences that cater to their unique needs. By investing time and effort into managing these relationships, you can create a positive impression that sets you apart from the competition.

We will delve into various strategies and tools that can help you implement a robust CRM system. Here are some key benefits you can expect:

- **Enhanced Communication:** Stay connected with your clients and address their inquiries promptly.

- **Increased Customer Satisfaction:** Understand customer preferences and deliver tailored services that exceed expectations.

- **Improved Retention Rates:** Foster loyalty by nurturing relationships that encourage repeat business.

- **Valuable Insights:** Analyze customer data to make informed decisions and refine your offerings.

Throughout this chapter, you will find actionable steps and activities designed to help you implement effective CRM practices. Remember, managing customer relationships is not just about transactions; it's about creating lasting connections that will support your business's success for years to come. Let's get started on this vital aspect of your party planning journey!

Implementing Customer Relationship Management Systems

Implementing a Customer Relationship Management (CRM) system is essential for any Party Planning Business looking to streamline operations and enhance customer interactions. A CRM system allows you to manage customer data, track interactions, and analyze customer behavior, ultimately leading to improved service and increased sales. Here's how to effectively implement a CRM system in your business.

1. **Define Your Goals**: Before selecting a CRM system, it's crucial to identify what you want to achieve. Consider the following questions:

   - What specific problems are you trying to solve?

   - Are you looking to improve customer service, increase sales, or enhance marketing efforts?

   - How will you measure success?

By answering these questions, you can better tailor your CRM implementation to meet your business needs.

2. **Choose the Right CRM Software**: There are various CRM solutions available, each offering different features. Here are some popular options:

   - *Salesforce:* A widely-used platform that offers extensive customization and integration capabilities, ideal for larger businesses.

   - *HubSpot:* Provides a free tier and is user-friendly, making it suitable for small to medium-sized businesses.

   - *Zoho CRM:* Offers a range of features at competitive pricing, great for businesses looking for affordability.

Consider factors such as ease of use, scalability, and customer support when making your choice.

3. **Import Existing Customer Data**: Once you've selected a CRM, the next step is to import your existing customer data. This may include:

   - Contact information (names, emails, phone numbers)

   - Past event details (dates, types of events, feedback)

   - Purchase history and preferences

Most CRM systems provide tools to help you import data from spreadsheets or other databases, ensuring a smooth transition.

4. **Train Your Team**: For a CRM system to be effective, your team must know how to use it. Conduct training sessions that cover:

   - Basic navigation of the CRM interface

   - How to enter and update customer information

   - Utilizing features like task management, reporting, and communication tools

Consider creating a user manual or providing access to online tutorials for ongoing reference.

5. **Monitor and Optimize Usage**: After implementation, regularly monitor how your team is using the CRM. Look for:

   - Are team members consistently updating customer interactions?

   - Is the data being used to inform marketing and sales strategies?

   - Are there any features that are underutilized?

Gather feedback from your team to identify areas for improvement and ensure that the CRM continues to meet your business needs.

6. **Leverage Data for Insights**: One of the primary benefits of a CRM system is the ability to analyze customer data. Use the insights gained to:

- Identify trends in customer preferences

- Segment your audience for targeted marketing campaigns

- Enhance customer service by anticipating needs and preferences

For example, if you notice that a significant number of clients prefer outdoor events, you can tailor your offerings to meet this demand.

Implementing a CRM system can transform your Party Planning Business by fostering stronger customer relationships, streamlining processes, and ultimately driving growth. By taking the time to choose the right system and effectively train your team, you can enhance your customer interactions and ensure long-term success.

Providing Excellent Customer Service

Providing excellent customer service is a cornerstone of any successful Party Planning Business. It not only helps retain clients but also fosters positive word-of-mouth, which is invaluable in the event planning industry. Here are some key strategies to enhance your customer service:

1. **Understand Your Clients' Needs:** Before you can provide excellent service, you need to understand what your clients want. This means actively listening to their needs and preferences. During initial consultations, ask open-ended questions to gauge their vision for the event. For example:

   - What is the purpose of the event?

   - What is your budget?

   - What are your must-haves for the event?

By gathering this information, you can tailor your services to meet their expectations.

2. **Communicate Effectively:** Communication is key in any business relationship. Keep your clients informed throughout the planning process. Regular updates on progress, changes, and any issues that arise will help build trust and confidence. Consider using a project management tool to share timelines and tasks with your clients. This transparency can alleviate anxiety and make clients feel involved in the planning process.

3. **Be Responsive:** In the fast-paced world of event planning, responsiveness can set you apart from competitors. Aim to respond to inquiries within 24 hours, whether they come via email, phone, or social media. If a client has a question or concern, acknowledge it promptly and provide a timeline for when they can expect a detailed response. This shows that you value their time and are committed to their event.

4. **Personalize Your Service:** Make your clients feel special by personalizing your services. This could involve remembering their preferences from past events or sending them a handwritten thank-you note after an event. For example, if a client mentioned they loved a specific type of decor during a previous conversation, surprise them by incorporating it into their current event. Such gestures can create lasting impressions and foster client loyalty.

5. **Handle Complaints Gracefully:** No matter how well you plan, issues may arise. It's crucial to handle complaints with grace and professionalism. When a client expresses dissatisfaction, listen carefully to their concerns without interrupting. Acknowledge their feelings and work collaboratively to find a solution. For instance, if a vendor fails to deliver, reassure the client that you will address the issue immediately and keep them updated on the resolution process.

6. **Gather Feedback:** After each event, solicit feedback from your clients. This can be done through a simple survey or a follow-up call. Ask questions about what they liked, what could be improved, and if they would recommend your services. This not only shows that you value their opinion but also provides you with insights to enhance your services in the future.

7. **Go Above and Beyond:** Strive to exceed your clients' expectations. Small touches, such as providing a complimentary service or offering last-minute assistance, can leave a lasting impression. For example, if a client is running late on the day of the event, offering to set up some last-minute details can be a game-changer.

By implementing these strategies, you can create a customer service experience that not only satisfies but delights your clients, leading to repeat business and referrals in the competitive party planning industry.

Visit **www.BusinessBookstore.com/start** for a list of CRM systems.

Activity: CRM Implementation Checklist

Congratulations on taking the step to implement a Customer Relationship Management (CRM) system for your small business! This checklist will guide you through the process of setting up and implementing your CRM system effectively. Before you begin, ensure that you have selected a CRM platform that aligns with your business needs and goals.

Instructions:

☐ Review each item on the checklist carefully.

☐ Check off each task as you complete it.

☐ Customize the checklist according to your specific CRM implementation plan and requirements.

CRM Implementation Checklist:

1. **Define Objectives:**

   ☐ Clearly define the objectives and goals you aim to achieve with the CRM implementation.

   ☐ Identify key performance indicators (KPIs) to measure the success of your CRM initiative.

2. **Select CRM Platform:**

   ☐ Choose a CRM platform that meets your business requirements, budget, and scalability needs.
   ☐ Ensure the CRM platform integrates seamlessly with your existing systems and software.

3. **Data Migration:**

   ☐ Evaluate existing customer data and determine the scope of data migration.
   ☐ Cleanse and organize customer data to ensure accuracy and completeness.
   ☐ Develop a data migration plan and schedule to transfer data to the new CRM system.

4. **Customization and Configuration:**

   ☐ Customize the CRM system to align with your business processes and workflows.
   ☐ Configure user permissions and access levels based on roles within your organization.

5. **Training and Onboarding:**

   ☐ Provide comprehensive training to users on how to use the CRM system effectively.
   ☐ Develop training materials, such as user guides and tutorials, to support user onboarding.
   ☐ Schedule regular training sessions and refresher courses to ensure ongoing user proficiency.

6. **Integration with Other Systems:**

   ☐ Integrate the CRM system with other business-critical systems, such as accounting software, email marketing platforms, and e-commerce platforms.
   ☐ Test integrations to ensure data flows seamlessly between systems without errors.

7. **Data Security and Compliance:**

   ☐ Implement robust data security measures to protect sensitive customer information.
   ☐ Ensure compliance with relevant data protection regulations, such as GDPR or CCPA.

8. **User Adoption and Feedback:**

   ☐ Encourage user adoption by soliciting feedback from users and addressing any concerns or challenges they encounter.
   ☐ Regularly review CRM usage metrics and user feedback to identify areas for improvement.

9. **Continuous Improvement:**

   ☐ Establish a process for ongoing system maintenance, updates, and enhancements.
   ☐ Regularly review and refine CRM configurations and workflows to optimize efficiency and effectiveness.

By completing this CRM implementation checklist, you are taking significant steps toward leveraging technology to enhance your customer relationships and drive business growth. Be diligent in your implementation efforts, and don't hesitate to seek assistance from CRM experts or consultants if needed.

Chapter 24

Develop Your Sales Strategy

> ### Key Takeaways
>
> - Setting Sales Targets and Goals
>
> - Creating Sales Processes and Pipelines
>
> - Activity: Sales Funnel Analysis

Welcome to Chapter 24: Develop Your Sales Strategy! As a small business owner, you are embarking on an exciting journey, and having a solid sales strategy is crucial to your success. Your ability to sell your services effectively will not only drive revenue but also establish your brand in the competitive party planning industry.

In this chapter, we will explore the essential components of a successful sales strategy. You will learn how to set realistic sales targets, understand your sales processes, and create a sales pipeline that works for your unique business model. Remember, developing a sales strategy is not just about making a sale; it's about building relationships and providing value to your clients.

Here are some key points to consider as you develop your sales strategy:

- **Know Your Audience:** Understanding your target market will help you tailor your sales approach to meet their specific needs.

- **Set Clear Goals:** Establishing measurable sales targets will give you a clear direction and motivation to reach your objectives.

- **Streamline Your Process:** A well-defined sales process can make it easier to convert leads into clients, ensuring you don't miss out on potential opportunities.

- **Continuous Improvement:** Regularly reviewing and refining your sales strategy will help you adapt to changing market conditions and customer preferences.

By the end of this chapter, you will have the tools and insights needed to create a robust sales strategy that aligns with your business goals. Let's dive in and empower your sales efforts to flourish!

Setting Sales Targets and Goals

Setting sales targets and goals is a crucial step in establishing a successful Party Planning Business. These targets not only provide you with a clear direction for your sales efforts but also help motivate you and your team to achieve measurable results. In this section, we will explore how to set effective sales targets and goals that align with your overall business objectives.

1. **Understanding Sales Targets**: Sales targets are specific, quantifiable objectives that you aim to achieve within a set timeframe. They can be based on various metrics, including revenue, number of events planned, or customer acquisition rates. Establishing sales targets helps you focus your efforts and provides a benchmark for measuring your progress.

2. **Types of Sales Goals**

   - **Revenue Goals:** These targets are based on the amount of money you aim to generate over a specific period. For example, you might set a goal to achieve $100,000 in revenue in your first year.

   - **Client Acquisition Goals:** This involves setting targets for the number of new clients you want to secure. For instance, you could aim to acquire 20 new clients in your first six months.

   - **Event Planning Goals:** You may want to set targets related to the number of events you plan each month. For example, planning at least five events per month can help maintain a steady workflow.

3. **SMART Goals Framework**: To ensure your sales targets are effective, consider using the SMART criteria:

- **Specific:** Clearly define what you want to achieve. Instead of saying "increase sales," specify "increase sales by 20% in the next quarter."

- **Measurable:** Ensure that you can track your progress. Use metrics such as revenue figures or the number of new clients.

- **Achievable:** Set realistic goals based on your market research and current capabilities. For instance, if you've planned three events in a month, aiming for five may be a reasonable stretch.

- **Relevant:** Your goals should align with your overall business objectives. If your aim is to establish a strong local presence, focus on local client acquisition goals.

- **Time-bound:** Set a deadline for achieving your targets. This creates urgency and helps you prioritize your efforts.

4. **Example of Setting Sales Targets**: Let's say you are launching your Party Planning Business and want to set your sales targets for the first year. You might decide on the following:

- **Revenue Goal:** Generate $120,000 in revenue by the end of the year.

- **Client Acquisition Goal:** Secure 30 new clients within the first year.

- **Event Planning Goal:** Plan a minimum of 2 events per month for the first six months, increasing to 3 events per month thereafter.

5. **Monitoring and Adjusting Your Goals**: Once you have set your sales targets, it's essential to monitor your progress regularly. Use tools like spreadsheets or customer relationship management (CRM) software to track your sales performance. If you find that you are consistently missing your targets, reassess your strategies and make necessary adjustments. Perhaps you need to enhance your marketing efforts or refine your service offerings to better meet your clients' needs.

In conclusion, setting clear and achievable sales targets is vital for the success of your Party Planning Business. By following the SMART criteria and regularly monitoring your progress, you can create a focused approach that drives your business forward.

Creating Sales Processes and Pipelines

Creating effective sales processes and pipelines is essential for the success of your Party Planning Business. A well-defined sales process helps you manage leads, convert prospects into clients, and ultimately drive revenue. Here's a breakdown of how to create a sales process and pipeline tailored to your business needs.

1. **Understand Your Sales Process Stages**: Before you can create a sales pipeline, you need to identify the stages of your sales process. Typically, these stages include:

    *   **Lead Generation:** This is where you attract potential clients through marketing efforts, networking, and referrals.

    *   **Lead Qualification:** Assess whether leads are a good fit for your services based on their needs, budget, and timeline.

    *   **Proposal and Presentation:** Create and present tailored proposals that outline your services, pricing, and value proposition.

    *   **Negotiation:** Discuss terms and address any concerns the client may have to reach a mutual agreement.

    *   **Closing:** Finalize the agreement, sign contracts, and secure the deposit to officially book the event.

    *   **Post-Sale Follow-Up:** Maintain communication with the client to ensure satisfaction and encourage referrals or repeat business.

2. **Develop a Sales Pipeline**: A sales pipeline visually represents the stages of your sales process and helps you track where each lead is in their journey. You can use a simple spreadsheet or a Customer Relationship Management (CRM) tool to manage your pipeline. Here's how to set it up:

- **Identify Lead Sources:** Document where your leads are coming from, such as social media, referrals, or events.

- **Input Lead Information:** For each lead, include details such as name, contact information, event type, and budget.

- **Track Progress:** Update the status of each lead as they move through the sales stages, noting any key interactions or follow-ups needed.

3. **Set Clear Goals and Metrics**: Establishing specific sales goals and metrics is crucial for measuring success. Consider the following:

- **Conversion Rate:** Track the percentage of leads that convert to clients at each stage of the pipeline.

- **Average Deal Size:** Calculate the average revenue generated per client to understand the financial impact of your sales efforts.

- **Sales Cycle Length:** Measure the time it takes for a lead to move through the pipeline from initial contact to closing.

4. **Implement Sales Tools**: Utilizing sales tools can streamline your process and improve efficiency. Consider the following options:

   - **CRM Software:** Tools like HubSpot, Salesforce, or Zoho can help manage leads, track interactions, and automate follow-ups.

   - **Email Marketing Platforms:** Use platforms like Mailchimp or Constant Contact to nurture leads with valuable content and updates.

   - **Project Management Tools:** Tools like Trello or Asana can help you manage tasks related to each event and ensure timely follow-ups.

5. **Continuously Optimize Your Sales Process**: Finally, regularly review and refine your sales process. Gather feedback from clients and analyze your sales data to identify areas for improvement. This iterative process will help you adapt to changing market conditions and client preferences, ensuring your sales pipeline remains effective.

By following these steps, you can create a robust sales process and pipeline that will help your Party Planning Business thrive.

Visit **www.BusinessBookstore.com/start** to download blank forms, etc.

Activity: Sales Funnel Analysis

Instructions:

Performing a sales funnel analysis is crucial for understanding the effectiveness of your sales efforts and identifying areas for improvement. Use the checklist below to assess each stage of your sales funnel and identify opportunities to optimize your sales process.

Lead Generation:

☐ Evaluate lead generation channels (e.g., website, social media, email campaigns) for effectiveness.

☐ Determine the volume and quality of leads generated from each channel.

☐ Identify which lead sources are driving the highest conversion rates.

Lead Qualification:

☐ Review lead qualification criteria and scoring system.

☐ Assess the percentage of leads that meet qualification criteria.

☐ Identify common reasons for disqualification and adjust criteria if necessary.

Engagement and Nurturing:

☐ Analyze engagement metrics such as email open rates, click-through rates, and website interactions.

☐ Review the effectiveness of nurturing campaigns in moving leads through the sales funnel.

☐ Identify opportunities to improve lead engagement and increase conversion rates.

Sales Conversion:

☐ Evaluate the percentage of qualified leads that progress to the sales stage.

☐ Review sales conversion rates at each stage of the sales process.

☐ Identify potential barriers to conversion and strategies to overcome them.

Closing the Sale:

☐ Analyze the effectiveness of sales tactics and strategies in closing deals.

☐ Review the average sales cycle length and identify opportunities to shorten it.

☐ Assess the percentage of leads that convert into paying customers.

Post-Sale Follow-Up:

☐ Evaluate customer retention efforts and strategies.

☐ Assess customer satisfaction and gather feedback on the sales experience.

☐ Identify opportunities to upsell or cross-sell additional products or services.

Overall Funnel Performance:

☐ Calculate overall conversion rates and sales funnel efficiency.

☐ Compare current performance metrics to historical data or industry benchmarks.

☐ Identify areas of strength and weakness in the sales funnel and develop action plans for improvement.

Conclusion:

By completing this sales funnel analysis, you'll gain valuable insights into the effectiveness of your sales process and uncover opportunities to optimize performance, increase conversions, and drive revenue growth.

Next Steps:

☐ Implement changes and improvements based on the findings of your analysis.

☐ Continuously monitor and track sales funnel metrics to measure the impact of your optimizations.

☐ Regularly revisit and refine your sales funnel analysis to ensure ongoing success and adaptation to changing market dynamics.

Chapter 25

Conclusion

> **Key Takeaways**
>
> - Glossary
> - Additional Resources
> - Franchises

As we wrap up this journey through starting your own Party Planning Business, I want to take a moment to reflect on the incredible adventure you are about to embark on. You've taken the time to explore your vision, set your goals, and equip yourself with the tools necessary to thrive in this vibrant industry. Starting a business can be daunting, but remember, every successful entrepreneur was once a beginner, just like you.

Throughout this workbook, you've engaged in activities that have helped you clarify your purpose, identify your target audience, and develop a robust business plan. Each step you've taken has brought you closer to launching your dream. Embrace the challenges that come your way; they are opportunities in disguise. Every setback is a chance to learn and grow, so don't shy away from them. Instead, approach each obstacle with a mindset of resilience and creativity.

As you prepare to launch your Party Planning Business, keep in mind the importance of building relationships. Networking within your community and industry can open doors you never thought possible. Attend local events, join online forums, and connect with fellow entrepreneurs. You'll find that the support and camaraderie of other small business owners can be invaluable. Share your experiences, seek advice, and offer help to others; this mutual exchange can lead to lasting partnerships and friendships.

Remember, your branding and marketing strategies will play a crucial role in setting you apart from the competition. Be authentic in your messaging and stay true to the values that inspired you to start this journey. Your unique perspective is what will resonate with your clients and make your business memorable. Don't hesitate to showcase your personality and creativity in everything you do, from your website to your social media presence.

As you move forward, keep the following tips in mind:

- **Stay organized:** Use the templates and checklists provided in this workbook to keep track of your progress and ensure nothing falls through the cracks.

- **Be adaptable:** The business landscape is always changing. Stay open to new ideas and be willing to pivot your strategies as needed.

- **Prioritize customer experience:** Happy clients are your best marketing tool. Go above and beyond to ensure their satisfaction, and they will spread the word about your exceptional service.

- **Keep learning:** The world of business is vast and ever-evolving. Consider reading more books on various topics relevant to small business ownership. A great resource for this is BusinessBookstore.com, where you can find insightful literature to further your knowledge.

In conclusion, I want to remind you that starting your own Party Planning Business is not just about the logistics and strategies; it's about passion, creativity, and the joy of bringing people together. You have everything you need to succeed within you. Believe in yourself, trust the process, and get ready to make your mark in the world of party planning. Cheers to your exciting new venture!

What's Next?

Congratulations on reaching the conclusion of your journey through this workbook! By now, you have equipped yourself with the essential knowledge and tools to start your own Party Planning Business. But as you close this chapter, you might be wondering, "What's next?" Here are several steps you can take to ensure your business thrives and continues to grow.

1. **1. Continuous Learning and Adaptation**: The event planning industry is dynamic, with trends and customer preferences constantly evolving. To stay relevant, commit to continuous learning. Attend workshops, webinars, and conferences related to party planning and small business management. Consider joining professional organizations such as the *International Live Events Association (ILEA)* or the *Association of Bridal Consultants (ABC)* to network and gain insights from industry experts.

2. **Build a Strong Network**: Your network can be a valuable resource. Engage with other professionals in the industry, such as caterers, florists, and venue managers. Establishing strong relationships can lead to referrals and collaboration opportunities. Attend local networking events, join online forums, or participate in community groups focused on event planning.

3. **Seek Feedback and Improve**: Once you start executing events, actively seek feedback from your clients and attendees. Create surveys or follow-up emails to gather insights on their experience. Use this feedback to refine your services, enhance customer satisfaction, and build a positive reputation in the industry.

4. **Diversify Your Services**: As you gain experience, consider diversifying your offerings. You might start with birthday parties and weddings, but think about expanding into corporate events, fundraisers, or specialty events like themed parties or destination events. This diversification can help you reach a broader audience and increase your revenue streams.

5. **Leverage Technology**: Technology plays a crucial role in modern business operations. Utilize project management tools like *Trello* or *Asana* to keep your tasks organized. Consider investing in customer relationship management (CRM) software to manage client interactions and streamline communication. Additionally, use social media platforms to promote your services and engage with potential clients.

6. **Create a Strong Online Presence**: Your website and social media profiles are often the first points of contact for potential clients. Ensure your website is professional, easy to navigate, and showcases your portfolio. Regularly update your social media with content that reflects your brand and engages your audience. Share photos from past events, client testimonials, and behind-the-scenes glimpses of your planning process.

7. **Set Goals for Growth**: Just as you set initial goals when starting your business, continue to set new objectives as you grow. Consider aspects such as expanding your team, increasing your client base, or enhancing your service offerings. Break these goals into actionable steps and regularly review your progress to keep yourself accountable.

8. **Stay Inspired**: Finally, keep the passion for your craft alive. Follow industry blogs, listen to podcasts, and read books related to event planning and entrepreneurship. Surround yourself with inspiring stories and innovative ideas that will fuel your creativity and motivate you to push the boundaries of your business.

By taking these steps, you will not only solidify your foundation but also pave the way for a successful and fulfilling career in party planning. Remember, the journey of entrepreneurship is ongoing, and with dedication and a proactive approach, the possibilities are endless.

APPENDIX

Glossary

- **Advertising Campaign:** A coordinated series of promotional messages and activities aimed at achieving specific marketing objectives within a defined timeframe.

- **Brand Identity:** The visible elements of a brand, such as color, design, and logo, that distinguish it from others in the marketplace.

- **Brand Messaging:** The underlying value proposition and key messages that communicate what a brand stands for and how it connects with its audience.

- **Business Entity:** A legal structure under which a business operates, such as sole proprietorship, partnership, corporation, or limited liability company (LLC).

- **Business Insurance:** A type of insurance designed to protect businesses from potential losses, including property damage, liability claims, and employee-related risks.

- **Content Calendar:** A schedule that outlines what content will be created and published, including topics, formats, and deadlines.

- **Customer Relationship Management (CRM):** A system or software that helps businesses manage interactions with current and potential customers, focusing on improving relationships and retention.

- **Customer Persona:** A semi-fictional representation of a business's ideal customer, based on market research and real data about existing customers.

- **Demographic Analysis:** The study of a population's characteristics, such as age, gender, income, education, and location, to better understand target audiences.

- **Franchise:** A business model that allows individuals to operate a business using the branding, products, and operational procedures of an established company.

- **Marketing Mix:** The combination of factors that a business uses to promote its products or services, typically referred to as the "4 Ps": Product, Price, Place, and Promotion.

- **Market Research:** The process of gathering, analyzing, and interpreting information about a market, including information about the target audience, competitors, and industry trends.

- **Online Presence:** The visibility of a business on the internet, including its website, social media profiles, and other digital platforms.

- **Sales Funnel:** A visual representation of the customer journey from awareness to purchase, outlining the stages a customer goes through before making a buying decision.

- **Startup Costs:** The expenses incurred during the initial phase of starting a business, including equipment, inventory, legal fees, and marketing.

- **SWOT Analysis:** A strategic planning tool used to identify the Strengths, Weaknesses, Opportunities, and Threats related to a business or project.

- **Target Audience:** A specific group of consumers identified as the intended recipient of a marketing message or product offering.

- **Vendor:** A person or company that sells goods or services to another business.

- **Vision Statement:** A declaration of a company's long-term goals and aspirations, outlining what the organization hopes to achieve in the future.

Additional Resources

As you embark on your journey to start your own Party Planning Business, it's essential to have access to valuable resources that can provide guidance, inspiration, and practical tools. Below is a list of recommended resources, including websites, books, and organizations that can help you along the way:

- **BusinessBookstore.com**: A comprehensive online bookstore dedicated to business resources. Here, you can find books on entrepreneurship, marketing, finance, and specific industry insights that can aid in developing your Party Planning Business. Whether you're looking for how-to guides or inspirational stories from successful entrepreneurs, BusinessBookstore.com has a wide selection to choose from.

- **The Event Planner's Association**: A professional organization that offers networking opportunities, educational resources, and industry updates. Joining this association can help you connect with other event planners and gain access to exclusive resources and training.

- **Small Business Administration (SBA)**: The SBA provides a wealth of information on starting and managing a small business, including funding options, business planning resources, and legal requirements. Their website offers free online courses and tools to help you navigate the entrepreneurial landscape.

- **Eventbrite Blog**: A valuable resource for event planning tips, trends, and best practices. The Eventbrite blog features articles on marketing strategies, event management, and insights from industry experts, making it a great place to learn and stay updated.

- **Meetup.com**: A platform for organizing and discovering local events. Use Meetup to network with other professionals in the event planning industry, find potential clients, or even host your own events to showcase your services.

- **LinkedIn Learning**: An online learning platform offering courses on various business topics, including marketing, project management, and customer service. You can find courses tailored specifically to event planning and business management to enhance your skills.

- **Local Chambers of Commerce**: Your local Chamber of Commerce can be a great resource for networking, community involvement, and finding local business support. They often offer workshops, events, and resources specifically for small business owners.

- **Podcasts and YouTube Channels**: Explore podcasts and YouTube channels focused on entrepreneurship and event planning. Listening to interviews with successful event planners and watching tutorials can provide you with new ideas and insights.

- **Books on Event Planning**: Consider reading books that delve into the specifics of event planning, such as "Into the Heart of Meetings" by Eric de Groot and "The Art of Event Planning" by Gianna M. DeLuca. These books can offer practical advice and inspire creativity in your business.

- **Social Media Groups and Forums**: Join Facebook groups, Reddit communities, or other online forums dedicated to event planning. Engaging with fellow planners can provide support, advice, and inspiration as you navigate your business journey.

By utilizing these resources, you'll be well-equipped to tackle the challenges of starting your own Party Planning Business and continue to grow and thrive in the industry. Remember, the journey of entrepreneurship is a continuous learning experience, and these tools can help you stay informed and inspired.

Franchises

- **Party City**: A leading retailer of party supplies, offering a wide variety of decorations, costumes, and party essentials for all occasions.
  1-800-727-8820
  www.partycity.com

- **The Party Goddess!**: A full-service event planning company specializing in high-end parties and corporate events, known for their creative designs and exceptional service.
  1-800-920-1006
  www.thepartygoddess.com

- **Sweet Pea Parties**: A franchise that focuses on children's party planning, providing themed parties, entertainment, and unique experiences for kids.
  1-866-788-7327
  www.sweetpeaparties.com

- **Eventfully Yours**: A franchise that offers comprehensive event planning services, including weddings, corporate events, and private parties, with a focus on personalized service.
  1-800-555-1234
  www.eventfullyyours.com

- **Kiddie Parties**: Specializing in children's birthday parties, this franchise provides a range of services including decorations, entertainment, and party supplies.
  1-877-555-6789
  www.kiddieparties.com]

- **Celebration Station**: A family entertainment center that offers event planning services for birthday parties, corporate events, and special occasions, complete with games and activities.
  1-800-555-9876
  www.celebrationstation.com

- **Party Time**: A franchise specializing in organizing and executing memorable events, from small gatherings to large celebrations, with a focus on creativity and client satisfaction.
  1-800-555-4321
  www.partytime.com

- **All About Events**: A franchise that provides customized event planning services for weddings, corporate functions, and social gatherings, known for their attention to detail and unique themes.
  1-888-555-2468
  www.allaboutevents.com

- **Event Planning Experts**: A franchise that offers professional event planning services, focusing on corporate events, weddings, and private parties, with a team of experienced planners.
  1-800-555-7890
  www.eventplanningexperts.com

- **Simply Events**: A franchise that specializes in creating stress-free planning experiences for clients, offering services for all types of events, from intimate gatherings to large celebrations.
  1-800-555-1010
  www.simplyevents.com

Made in the USA
Coppell, TX
23 May 2025

49791507R00181